The Bridge to I Am

The Bridge to I Am

✦

Rapid Advance Psychotherapy

Ellie Izzo, PhD

iUniverse, Inc.
New York Lincoln Shanghai

The Bridge to I Am
Rapid Advance Psychotherapy

Copyright © 2007, 2008 by Ellie Izzo

All rights reserved. No part of this book may be used or reproduced by any means, graphic, electronic, or mechanical, including photocopying, recording, taping or by any information storage retrieval system without the written permission of the publisher except in the case of brief quotations embodied in critical articles and reviews.

iUniverse books may be ordered through booksellers or by contacting:

iUniverse
2021 Pine Lake Road, Suite 100
Lincoln, NE 68512
www.iuniverse.com
1-800-Authors (1-800-288-4677)

Because of the dynamic nature of the Internet, any Web addresses or links contained in this book may have changed since publication and may no longer be valid.

The information, ideas, and suggestions in this book are not intended as a substitute for professional advice. Before following any suggestions contained in this book, you should consult your personal physician or mental health professional. Neither the author nor the publisher shall be liable or responsible for any loss or damage allegedly arising as a consequence of your use or application of any information or suggestions in this book.

ISBN: 978-0-595-46892-8 (pbk)
ISBN: 978-0-595-70602-0 (cloth)
ISBN: 978-0-595-91181-3 (ebk)

Printed in the United States of America

This Book is dedicated
to my husband and soul mate,
John Izzo.

Contents

ACKNOWLEDGEMENTS................................ ix
CHAPTER 1   INTRODUCTION 1
CHAPTER 2   THE SPIRITUAL BRIDGE.................... 9
CHAPTER 3   REVEALING THE HISTORY 21
CHAPTER 4   RECOGNIZING THE IMPASSE............. 33
CHAPTER 5   RELEASING THE PAST..................... 43
CHAPTER 6   RESPONDING TO FEAR.................... 59
CHAPTER 7   RECONNECTING TO THE SPIRIT 77
CHAPTER 8   THE SPIRITUAL ALLIANCE................. 87
CHAPTER 9   THE PRACTICE OF BRIDGING: A REVIEW ... 93
CHAPTER 10   A RATIONALE FOR THE
                    PROFESSIONAL......................... 101
CHAPTER 11   REFERENCES 113
ABOUT THE AUTHOR 119

ACKNOWLEDGEMENTS

The evolution of this theory has been many years in the making. I would like to acknowledge and thank all the brilliant practitioners and researchers in the field of psychotherapy and counseling. Their contribution has been paramount to the development of this book. I want to acknowledge that all chapter subtitles have been adapted from <u>A Course in Miracles</u>. If I have failed to cite an appropriate source, I am truly sorry.

I also want to thank my clients and remind readers that all case studies and names are fictitious, but based on bits and pieces of clients' stories that have been so valuable to my growth and understanding of human nature.

Lastly, I want to thank my husband and family who help give my life the meaning and dimension so necessary for loving beliefs.

1

INTRODUCTION

All power is of your God, what is not of Him has no power to do anything.

You have a higher mind. Everyone does. It is located in the upper prefrontal cortex of the brain. The ability to access the higher mind takes time, volition, and attention (Begley 2007). Many of us are so caught up in the minutia of stressful living we forget about this option. There are mental states such as happiness, enthusiasm, compassion, joy, and other positive emotions housed in the upper left brain that are easier to elicit and can last longer with spiritual practice. We are very busy trying to control all the details of our lives and forget about taking charge of our inner well-being by accessing our higher mind. Pity, because that inner well-being is the starting point for how we make relationships.

There is essentially only one kind of relationship and that is a spiritual alliance. Anything else is actually no relationship at all. Anything other than a spiritual alliance is simply collaboration in fear. Fear is our devil. It is our devil because it is the force of separation. Fear leads to judgmental thinking about oneself and then, others. This judgmental thinking separates countries, states, cities, corporations, neighborhoods, families, couples and it separates individuals from their true powerful Selves. This Self can be called the **I Am**. The **I Am** is the Self that is connected to the Higher Mind or God. This Self knows no separation. God is Love and Love erases fear into the nothingness it really is. Free from fear and the seductiveness of judgmental thinking, the **I Am** is detached from the painful past, unperturbed about tomorrow and peacefully centered in the present.

Everything I have learned about conducting effective psychotherapy over the past thirty years has culminated in teaching my clients how to build healing and empowering relationships or spiritual alliances. This can only be realized by building an inner relationship or bridging to the Higher Mind, the **I Am**. The goal of the five-step process described in this book is based largely on my study of neuroscience and diverse spiritual teachings. The gap between science and spirit continues to significantly diminish, as research demonstrates the power of neuroplasticity in the human brain. An individual can literally rewire the unhealthy circuitry of neuroanatomy by training the mind. Studies demonstrate that people who practice spirituality with free will and concentration can produce neurogenesis, the birth of new neural circuitry, so that they can access the high left prefrontal cortex, the cerebral area associated with happiness and joy (Begley, 2007).

The spiritual perspective offers us the option of healing our minds and improving the neural circuitry of our brain through exchanging our emotional purpose. We give the unconscious, lower brain purpose of *projecting fear* over to the Higher Mind and in so doing, we bridge to the **I Am**, a present state of consciousness where self-judgment is suspended. We are most powerful in this state because when we are totally accepting of our Selves, we can extend Love. When we extend Love, we also *receive* it. We are confident, creative, courageous, trustful and hopeful. We exchange fear for Love and we are recovered.

While the five step process is derived from my professional and personal integration of the work of many renowned and some obscure experts in the fields of neuroscience and spirituality, my most beneficial learning experiences have been through my clients. Some of their stories are recounted in this book with names and details changed to protect confidentiality. The thousands of people I've worked with have taught me that being fearful and separated is disguised by different symptoms and therefore, different diagnoses. Once the disguise is peeled away, most clients report the same existential upset of separation and abandonment. They see themselves as unworthy of Love. They struggle with giving it. And, they struggle with getting it. I call the different symptoms and diagnoses, *distractions* from the core issue of being stuck somewhere in their inherent human ability to bridge to the **I Am**.

As the world continues to reflect a profound state of spiritual crisis through fear, judgment, and the consequence of separation, people are thinking about Love and considering their definition of God. We are tired of being afraid because we are anxious and so lonely with the isolation and abandonment that prevails when we are separated. We read the papers, watch the news, go to work, talk to other people and there it is … hatred, plague, famine, rape, war. The Book of Revelation calls this the Apocalypse. It is really saddening to watch how people tend to treat themselves and each other. We are ready and in need to build spiritual alliances. These are very powerful, healing relationships and their loving energy radiates throughout many other surrounding affiliations. They resemble the circular configuration one sees when a pebble is dropped into a stream. The pebble itself symbolizes the individual who has affected an inner relationship with Love, the **I Am**. A spiritual alliance is conceived first from within an individual and then exponentially ripples outward into eternity, passing through many relationship dimensions as it goes. We deserve to experience the peace, joy and power that Love creates in all of our relationships.

The spiritual perspective is our greatest and always abundant Natural Resource. A Natural Resource won't do you very much good unless you draw upon it. You can't draw from it unless you can link up to it and the attachment to the **I Am**, Spirit, or your personal God is via the **Spiritual Bridge**. The Spiritual Bridge is an inner awareness or consciousness that conjoins healthy, loving thoughts into healthy, loving beliefs. These loving beliefs translate outwardly into healthy, loving behaviors.

The Spirit is a part of the human personality you can't see. There are other parts of the personality you can't see: the intellectual and the emotional selves are not visible to the eye, yet we recognize they are there. The physical self is the only part of the self that can be seen, which is perhaps why humans place so much importance on it. The physical self is basically what you look like, the intellectual self is what you think about, the emotional self is what you feel, and the spiritual self is what you believe. What you believe will strongly affect every other part of your personality and will dictate how you will behave to yourself and to others.

A spiritual approach is to ask yourself, what are the objects of your faith? For instance, if you judge someone as dangerous, you will behave accordingly. You might avoid the person or attack him in an attempt to ward him off. In this case, fear is the object of your faith. Another possibility: if you judge that you are in some way defective, you will behave accordingly. You might never let anyone get really close to you; you might steer clear of him or attack him in an attempt to ward him off. Once again, fear is the object of your faith. Still another possibility—if you accept that you are worthy and valuable, you will behave accordingly. You will take risks and lovingly extend yourself to others. In this case, Love is the object of your faith.

When fear is the object of your faith, you not only isolate from others, you remain separate from your Spiritual Self and are therefore powerless to draw upon its power. You are alone. When Love is the object of your faith, you are linked up to the greatest Natural Resource and therefore empowered for winning relationships.

People who have a strong connection to the **Spiritual Self** tend to build belief systems upon creativity, enthusiasm, courage, hope, and trust. They feel a part of a higher order of things, have a sense of purpose and regard life as a gift that teaches us many valuable lessons. People who are disconnected from the Spirit tend to build belief systems upon an underlying sense of threat, internal conflict about their competence and adequacy, avoidance of important life challenges and a perception of themselves as victims. They believe life is hell on earth and they tend to produce a lot of pain and anguish for themselves and for those around them.

What are your beliefs? What are the objects of your faith? Do you believe it is every man for himself or do you espouse that you can be empowered by uniting with others? Do you give credence to a dog-eat-dog world or do you believe that every relationship blesses you and the other with an opportunity to grow and attract abundance into your respective lives? The human belief system is borne out of the Spirit and in order to examine your beliefs, you will have to consider the Spiritual Self.

If someone grows up disconnected from his Spirit, he will ultimately go on to unknowingly enable others to sever from the Spiritual Self and soon this existential suffering expands on a much greater sociological scale. Let's refrain from grandiosity right now. The idea of fixing the world is far too overwhelming. If individuals mended their Spiritual Bridge, they simultaneously would be making a global change as a natural consequence. Living with a broken Bridge as a distinct individual, can do you at worst, irreparable harm and at best, inhibit you from realizing your true gifts and talents. What can it do in the worst case? It can make you mentally ill, physically impaired, emotionally bankrupt and alone. What can it do in the best case? It can make you anxious, angry, afraid, shameful and lonely. In between those extremes you can find hostility, drug and alcohol abuse, sex addiction, eating disorders, laziness, passive aggression, apathy, depression, prejudice, brainwashing and assorted other "neuroses".

Rapid Advance Psychotherapy is a process that will quickly have you reconnect with your Spiritual Self, the **I Am**. You will remember your own inherent human ability to lead a healthy, wealthy, joyful, productive life. How does it do this? By empowering you to correct your belief system through the identification of how you initially incurred "breaks" in your Spiritual Bridge, how you perpetuate the "breaks" in the here and now and how you can reconnect with the Spiritual Self, which is the most powerful part of the human experience.

Once you have achieved an inner relationship with the Spiritual Self, you can draw upon the greatest Natural Resource. You can change the object of your faith and fear won't be your choice, because fear is not of the Spirit. Creativity, courage, confidence, hope, and trust are of the Spirit and serve as the foundation for healthy belief systems. Healthy belief systems are the building blocks for joyful relationships or spiritual alliances. The best part is that there is nothing you need to acquire outside of yourself, nothing to search for, and nothing to buy. Everything you need, you've had all along. You've simply forgotten that your Spiritual Self is there.

Let's face it, it's easy to forget. The other selves take up so much of our time and energy. The physical self is totally intrusive. We seem to be a very visually oriented society. The media has imposed that looking good and being physically fit is the key to success. The intellectual self has many of us over-thinking things so that we pay less and less attention to our "gut" or intuition. The emotional self has been the subject of endless volumes of writing. It appears that people are either not having their feelings or having too much of them. This is not to intimate that these parts of the personality are not meaningful and important. Quite the contrary, they are very important. However, when the physical, intellectual, and emotional selves are our focus at the sacrifice of the Spiritual Self, then we are operating out of balance, out of a faulty belief system, and we ultimately cause adversity for ourselves and others.

Rapid Advance Psychotherapy (RAP) is an accelerated form of therapy or personal growth through mending the Spiritual Bridge. If we accept that negative or frightening childhood experiences do their most extensive damage on a spiritual level, and since that is the greatest part of a child's psyche open to injury, **RAP** illustrates how an individual matures into adulthood with various "breaks" in their Spiritual Bridge.

The Spiritual Bridge is the part of the Spiritual Self that connects what one knows in their head to be true with what they believe in their heart, and ultimately goes on to live out in the present. A simplistic example is the behavior of smoking. Everyone knows that smoking can kill you. Still, some people smoke. They are unable to integrate what they know about the dangers of smoking into their behavior patterns, so they can refrain from the habit. A break or an impasse in the Spiritual Bridge prohibits the integration of thoughts and beliefs into healthy, loving behaviors. It is not unlike the spinal cord connecting the brain to the body. If there is a break in the cord, no matter how much you want to move an affected limb, it is just not going to happen!

SPIRITUAL BRIDGE

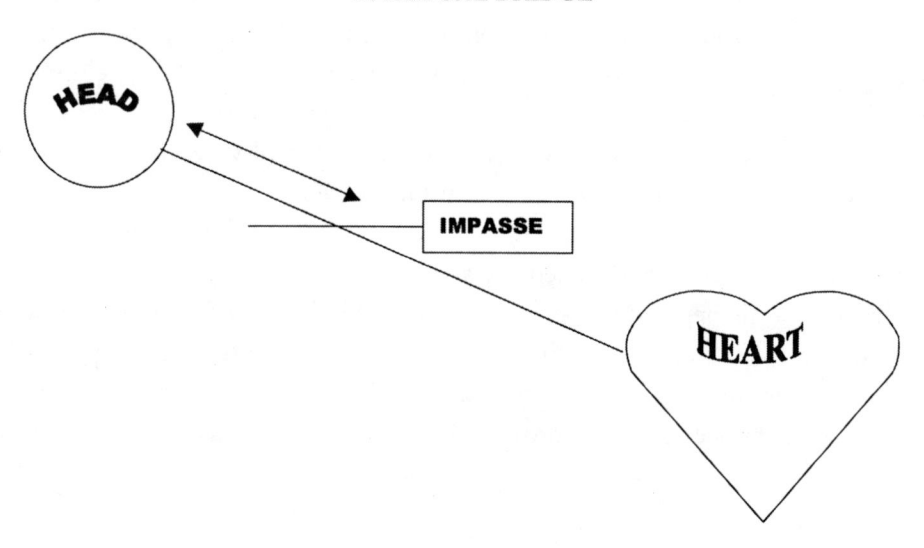

```
HEAD ←————————
         ————→ [IMPASSE]
                    ————————
                              HEART
```

His Holiness, the Dalai Lama (1997) stated that "love, compassion and tolerance are necessities, not luxuries. Without them, humanity cannot survive." Humans need spiritual sustenance. Without it, we find it difficult to get and maintain peace of mind. A good brain and a good heart should work together. The two must be developed in balance, and when they are, the result is material progress accompanied by good spiritual development (Dalai Lama 1997).

The goal of mending the Spiritual Bridge and enriching the inner relationship with the Spiritual Self is reached in a five step, accelerated process. The five steps comprise a psychotherapeutic experience. Now before you close your mind and then the book; stop and consider your beliefs about psychotherapy. What are some common misconceptions about psychotherapy? Psychotherapy is for crazy people. Psychotherapy is a crutch that sustains dependency among the weak. Psychotherapy is a financial rip-off that takes years to complete. These misconceptions are most tenaciously maintained by those who hold fear as the object of their faith, since people tend to fear the unknown and want to avoid that unpleasant feeling.

The **Rapid Advance** technique is a wellness model that assumes people are not sick; they are simply operating without the necessary information.

The information is nothing new. In fact, it is probably the oldest information in the world. It has simply been forgotten. *RAP* is an expeditious five step technique that supplies the valuable information. *RAP* is an enlightening alternative to a lengthy, costly therapeutic process. Again, you are quite functional and can easily assimilate the content. Everyone deserves to know. To have the information is your God-given right.

Once an individual has effected an inner transition from a fear-based to a Love-based perspective called the **I Am**, he/she is improving the neurocircuitry of his/her brain, operating from the Higher Mind, and is empowered to form fulfilling, enriching relationships of integrity. These spiritual alliances are healing and reciprocal in design and through them, the individual experiences growth and joy. Anything else is actually no relationship at all. Are you ready for love?

2

THE SPIRITUAL BRIDGE

Love, which created me, is what I am.

I Am is a complete thought. It is a thought established in the present. Being in the present is the only peaceful and powerful place to be. The essence of being with one's God is individually experienced on this earth by being in the present or in the **I Am**. The present is the earthly experience of eternity because the present is not constrained by the limited human concept of time. A Course in Miracles calls this the "holy instant" (Schucman & Thetford, 1975). I call it your moment of truth. The past and the future are constrained by time. A worldly definition of the **I Am** seems to be impossible, since the experience of it is beyond our worldly ability to confine its description by words. My understanding is that everyone's **I Am** is sacred onto itself and while it may be by individuals, experienced differently, **I Am** serves a single purpose of extending Love.

It is reported in the Hebrew Scriptures that Moses asked God, "When I go the people, who shall I say sent me?" God replied, "I Am that I Am. You must tell them: 'the one who is called **I Am** has sent me to you.'" The **I Am, Spiritual Perspective, Higher Mind,** and **God in You** are used synonymously in this book. They all refer to an inner level of consciousness based in peaceful self-acceptance.

In my personal and professional experiences, I have heard very few, including myself, simply state through their behaviors, "I Am." Instead, I hear "I am mad," "I am fat," "I am stupid," "I am ugly," "I am depressed," "I am the greatest" (which implies the existence of "I am the worst"), "I am a victim." Many seem to live by a code that dictates one can only say "I am" if it is followed by some word of judgment about who that is.

We appear to be a society of judge and jury, first onto ourselves and then onto others. We start out with, "I am in some way defective" and then move to "You are in some way defective." Judgment, which is predicated in the past and dictates the future, prohibits us from being in the now and one with our Higher Mind. When we are in the **I Am**, we are at peace and judgment becomes meaningless. We are empowered to access dynamics like creativity, confidence, courage, hope, trust and faith in oneself. We see ourselves rise above any worldly challenge. Being totally in the present, one with our personal concept of God, peaceful and powerful, requires a clear Spiritual Bridge. This inner consciousness is the unobstructed, two-way span that delivers judgmental thoughts to our God mind and God to our judgmental thoughts. Many individuals appear to have gaps or impasses in their Bridge. Forgiveness mends these impasses. Forgiveness, the relinquishment of judgment followed by a thought of peace, restores the individual's Spiritual Bridge to the **I Am**.

Spirituality is very popular these days. Pop spiritual books enjoy remaining at the top of the bestseller lists for lengthy amounts of time. We are demonstrating an enthusiasm to explore the spiritual realm and there is a lot of information out there discussing the nature of spirituality, but exactly how does one get there? It seems clear that we are ready to be with a sense of spiritedness or **I Am**, yet we have no sense about how to reach it and remain there. I have heard many of my clients, associates, and loved ones complain that they seem to get the hang of it for a while, but then get off track, forget about it, or get frustrated with staying connected. They see themselves as not yet skilled enough to get back quickly to **I Am**. The **Spiritual Bridge** provides that pathway. Mending the **Spiritual Bridge**, for many, is a requirement before they can relate to a concept of God.

This book will take you through five steps to access a clear, consistent connection to the Spirit. Our goal is to mend the Spiritual Bridge, which connects our head to our heart. The steps or the five **R's** are: 1) Revealing the History; 2) Recognizing the Impasse; 3) Releasing the Past; 4) Responding to Fear; and, 5) Reconnecting to the Spirit. Once you have become skilled in each step, you can quickly utilize them in different combinations in your daily life.

A spiritual alliance is an outward expansion of a restored inner **Spiritual Bridge**. First, the individual reconnects to his spiritual Self and once he has effected the inner connection, he is ready and compelled to extend this loving energy to others. Spiritual alliances can make life with a partner intimate and fruitful. They can make the workplace an integrated system of productivity and exuberance. Parenting becomes a charm instead of a chore. Friendships deepen into meaningful havens for regard and acceptance. A spiritual alliance heals old hurts, keeps us peacefully focused on the here and now, offers hope for the future and equally serves the participants. Many of us, at first, require individual training in order to clearly tap into the **I Am**, so that we may build these awesome relationships. Training includes restoring the pathway to the Higher Mind through a psychotherapeutic experience. This book offers you exactly that opportunity.

The state of your **Spiritual Bridge** is reflected in how you connect or attach to the world. If we were connected spirit-to-spirit, the world would be a very different place and a much nicer place for sure. Connection to the Spiritual Self is the first relationship and the paradigm for all others to follow. Your entire life experience can actually be understood as a series of attachments or relationships and your perception of these relationships is strongly affected by the nature of your inner spiritual relationship or lack thereof. If you don't have a clear connection to the Spirit, you are probably substituting a connection to something else; something that feels more familiar, even if it doesn't feel good. Those who have forgotten about the option of building an inner relationship to the Higher Mind generally substitute inner connections with negative feelings and will then *project* those negative feelings onto their worldly attachments. A worldly attachment can be a person, place, thing, or thought.

When we project onto a person, we take some judgment we have made about ourselves and then pass it along to the other. For example, the statement, "I am unworthy" can translate into, "You are mean to me." Usually, people will unconsciously adopt the sort of attachments utilized in their families of origin simply because that is familiar to them and they are also accustomed to the unpleasant feeling states that go along with the familiar historical attachments (Karen, 1998). Here's an example.

Tom came to into therapy in the midst of what I call an existential crisis. He was experiencing extreme anxiety and was tearful throughout the session. The presenting problem was that he had broken up with his girlfriend two days prior and shortly thereafter began to notice a sense of abandonment and loss. He felt disconnected and described his state, "like being sucked into a black hole, never to return from a dark abyss." That's what I call an existential crisis.

He had an on again, off again "relationship" with his girlfriend for two years. When she was interested and available to Tom, Tom wanted to party with his friends and have no commitments. When she was stand-offish, he went after her fervently and wanted to get married. His girlfriend would rage at him, criticize him, and threaten him about his mixed messages. The last time they did this dance, Tom broke up with her as an immediate way to stop her attack. Once she was unavailable to him, he went into crisis, perceiving himself as abandoned, at the entry of the black hole, and out of control. But instead of running back to her and promising her the world as usual, Tom did something different. He called me.

What we recognized, once we revealed his history, was that when Tom was little, he would act incorrigibly to get some attention until his mother got mad. After she got mad, she would ignore him for days. Tom recalled being terrified during those days of silent treatment. He was treated invisibly through being ignored. He perceived himself to be disconnected and abandoned. He received the experience as a break to his **Spiritual Bridge**. He felt terrified during those times and after promising his mother that he would be a very good boy a number of times, she would resume interacting with him. This was an unpleasant chain of events, but Tom got used to this form of attachment. He became so accustomed to it, he collaborated with another to experience it again. The existential crisis felt awful and it felt familiar. He went back and forth, from "I am ignored and alone" to "You are an abandoning person". Tom projected a painful piece of his history onto his girlfriend. She did the same with him.

There are many of us who can relate with the concept of being avoidant or being anxious when we are in a relationship. Some people feel afraid of the natural conflict inherent in all relationships and they avoid having these important interactions. The relationship suffers as a result. Others become anxious when in a relationship. They feel afraid they will be left and so they behave in a clingy, controlling, or intrusive manner. The relationship suffers as a result.

Impasses in the Spiritual Bridge render it useless. When we cannot bridge to our Higher Mind on the inside, we resort to projecting painful feelings as a way to connect on the outside. When we inwardly bridge to the **I Am**, we can outwardly give and receive Love freely. We have commonly accepted from the tenets of contemporary psychology that we need to love ourselves before we can love others. I believe we need to accept a personal sense of God's love before we can love others. An impasse in our Spiritual Bridge keeps us fearful that we are unworthy of Love. An unobstructed Bridge opens our consciousness for this acceptance. Those well trained in compassion meditation are well skilled in linking to the Higher Mind and achieving this peaceful state (Begley, 2007). This can be you!

Let's first talk about how psychotherapy helps us get there. Effective psychotherapy corrects how an individual connects to the world and it does this by focusing on two things. First, the psychotherapist gives healthy, empowering information to the client. Second, she/he extends her/his own inner connection to the Spiritual Self by building a spirit-to-spirit alliance with the client. The client leaves the experience empowered to build her/his own inner spiritual relationship, and ultimately projects that Love-based connection onto her/his outer relationships. The client is then able to correct perceptions of life experiences and connect to the world through Love.

Some of the most important material shared in psychotherapy is information about the feelings. There are many people who have little or no information about the emotional self and the feelings that are generated from that part (Burns, 1999). One thing I can assure you; if you don't have your feelings, they will have you in one form or another. I tend to categorize the feelings into a group which includes: mad, sad, glad, scared and ashamed. Mad and ashamed are offspring of scared. There are some eloquent feeling words such as frustrated, despondent, contented, intimidated and embarrassed. They can all be simplified to the first five. Notice that love is ***not*** one of the five feelings. That is because love is not a feeling; it is a process that includes effective control of the five feelings. The Spiritual Self is the most efficient feeling coach. If we are not in control of our feelings, they are in control of us and they become the agents through which we connect to the world.

Some people who connect to the world through anger, fear and shame walk around in a chronic state of anxiety, and aggress upon those around them. Here's an interesting example.

> I worked with a fifty-seven year old client named Ron. He was a nice enough real estate broker on the outside, but connected to the world through anger on the inside. On his first visit, he gave the receptionist a hard time about the scheduling of his appointment. On the second visit, he gave the insurance person a hard time about the billing procedures, and on the third visit he gave me a hard time about the length of my sessions. Ron really wanted help, but he connected to the world through anger and that is how he tried to start a relationship with me. Sometimes it was hard for me not to feel frustrated with Ron. You see, when someone connects to you with anger, they are inviting you to connect back in anger. Ron did this with just about everyone he met: the bank teller, the cashier, the telephone operator, motorists, attorneys and doctors. By the time Ron got to the therapeutic doorstep, he was failing in his career, he was claiming personal bankruptcy, he was sexually impotent, his wife of 37 years was divorcing him, his children had no respect for him, and Ron wanted to argue about the bill. Ron was desperate to connect—the more desperate he became, the angrier he became. When he walked through my door, I looked him in the eye and said, "Wow, you must really be suffering." Ron started to cry.

Ron was unmistakably broken in his Spiritual Bridge. Ron was raised by a very angry woman who was clearly disconnected from her spiritual Self, long before Ron was a thought. When he was five years old, unbeknownst to him, his mother was pregnant. Shortly before the new baby arrived, His mother dropped Ron off at an orphanage and did not return for over six months.

One day Ron was playing in the yard of the orphanage when through the fence, he saw his mother's car pull up to a store across the street. His mother got out of the car and pulled from it a baby girl, who she carried with her into the store. You certainly don't have to be Freud to figure out what must have been going through Ron's mind as he stood by the fence.

Ron's mother picked him up about four months later. Ron became disconnected from his spiritual Self clearly at an early age. Ron then began to connect to the world through anger. Fear was the object of his faith. He repeated to himself, "I am incompetent and I am a victim." He built a belief system based on underlying threat; people were out to get him; he could count on being betrayed; trust was never an option. As a result of his anger attachment, he believed he himself could not be trusted either. He lived this out in most every aspect of his life. And, unknowingly, through the break in his Spiritual Bridge, he broke the spirit of others. And with all that, no one was suffering as badly as Ron. You see, when we mistreat someone else, we are spiritually abusing ourselves. Ron was a collaborator in fear.

Psychotherapy had to be a healing experience for Ron. It had to mend the break in Ron's Spiritual Bridge, so that ultimately he would be able to reframe his angry perception of the world. He would connect to the world through Love. Psychotherapy is not about insanity. It is about learning to mend a Spiritual Bridge through the information and the role modeling provided by an effective therapist. It was my job to help Ron accept **God in him**, the **I Am**, and my method was to demonstrate how that is done via the spiritual alliance I would build with him. I let Ron know early, that I was not available to collaborate in fear and anger. I was enthused about connecting through love and I was excited to show him how.

Psychotherapy is a spirit-to-spirit alliance. It is learning to love, starting from within. Loving is extremely hard to do without a clear connection to the Spiritual Self. When someone is separated from the Spiritual Self, he does not see himself as lovable or valuable and he will engage in behaviors which are a cry for the help and the love he does not believe he deserves.

Some people who connect to the world through fear, anger and shame walk around in a chronic state of tension and avoid people around them.

> I worked with a fifty-two year old woman, Maria, married thirty-four years, with two married children. Maria held a high managerial position for a government agency. She had worked for the government since she was twenty and had accrued all the benefits that went with the longevity of her civil service. Maria was highly respected for the quality of her work; she was extremely fastidious and meticulous with the statistical, regulatory nature of her job. Unfortunately, Maria wasn't on the job very much. She was chronically ill with asthma and had to take two leaves of absence due to hospitalization for clinical depression. Maria had spent exorbitant amounts of time and money being treated for either physical or mental illness. When she was younger and raising her children, she could usually be found in bed or on the living room sofa. Outside people were called in to help with the kids. She had no friends, no hobbies and hardly left home except to go to work. The house was usually a mess and the grown children carried the scars of living with an unavailable mother.
>
> Maria lived in a town one hour away from my office. She originally set her therapy up to be conducted over the phone. As soon as I got some background, I stipulated that therapy would only be conducted in person. Maria did not want to show her face. She was desperate to connect and wanted to connect through shame. I was only available to have a connection through love. After canceling a number of appointments, Maria was feeling bad enough to make the drive and come in for a session. During that session, Maria revealed to me that she was the second daughter of an alcoholic, violent father. Her mother lived in trepidation of this man and did whatever she had to do to appease

him. Maria shared a room with her older sister and one night, when Maria was about eight years old, her father came into the room, drunk and belligerent. He then proceeded to rape her older sister, while Maria watched in horror. This scenario repeated many times, for many years.

Eventually, Her father would send her mother in to bring him the older sister. Her mother, in fear for her life, complied. Eventually, the older sister got pregnant and gave birth to a son, who was raised by Maria's mother as if he were her own. Maria got pregnant out of wedlock at eighteen and took off to marry the father of her child.

When Maria came in for therapy, she had just learned that her husband was having a long term extramarital affair. She was addicted to prescription medication. Her older sister was seriously ill and housed in a nursing home. Maria suffered an emotional setback every time she went to visit her.

Maria began interacting with the world through shame at an early age. She was very withdrawn in school, never took part in any activities, had no friends, and was considered to be a tomboy. As an adult, she wore very matronly clothes, no make-up, and a very antiquated hairstyle. She saw herself as a victim, unable to function. She sobbed throughout that first session and repeated that her life was awful and she simply wanted to end it all. Maria was seriously broken in her Spiritual Bridge and fear was clearly the object of her faith.

After entering into a no-suicide contract, we immediately began the mending process. It didn't take long to recognize that despite all the horror, the biggest source of her present shame was a misconstrued, persistent, belief that she was the unfavored child since her father never chose to have sex with her! She was consumed with self hatred as an adult because of this twisted judgment. She repeated to herself, "I am unchosen and disappointed." She began to heal quickly when she heard the loving feedback that it was normal for her to think that way as a child in an insane situation. You see, it was not so much the events themselves that caused Maria's struggle; it was her perception or judgment of them that truly had her stuck.

Ron and Maria present some intense examples of how we learn early to unconsciously collaborate in fear. While many of us cannot identify with such extreme experiences, we can certainly recognize the resulting behavior styles of connecting through anger and anxiety or attaching through avoidance and shame. While we may begin a relationship with the intent to operate from Love, we may tend with regularity to leave or separate ourselves from the relationship through anxiety or avoidance. We have all received some prior, rigorous training in collaborating in fear and over time, many of us have become quite skilled at it. Like riding a bike, once you get the hang of it, you do it automatically. Even if you haven't ridden in a while, you always remember how.

As a function of all the energy gone into this profitless training, our brains become neuro-wired in a fearful pattern and very little energy remains for learning something more beneficial and bountiful. Training for a spiritual alliance initially requires mending the Spiritual Bridge, thereby conserving the loving energy that has been draining away through self-judgment and the force of separation. Discovering and repairing where it began to leak out makes the remainder of the training a breeze to complete.

Not unlike Ron and Maria, many adults are wounded children. We can become constipated with our core of shame. Traditional psychotherapy and self-help have focused on it for years. Wounded children are quite simply, at an impasse in their Spiritual Bridge. They grow into adults who are separated from their Higher Mind. They then form collaborations, where they unconsciously help maintain the impasse in the Spiritual Bridges of themselves and others. Eric Berne (1964), developer of Transactional Analysis, might describe this as "I am not OK, so you are not OK." This is the antithesis of the natural design of the universe. Unless a relationship is healing and nurturing to the spirit, it is no relationship at all. There are a lot of us out there who are kidding ourselves.

When couples take their wedding vows, "... to have and to hold, to love and to cherish, for better or worse, for richer or poorer, in sickness and health, until death do us part," they are promising to unite in spirit. Sadly, they break the promise and deny themselves all the gifts a marital union has to offer. They could be delighting in closeness, success, and wealth. Instead, they settle for pain, resentment and loss.

Similarly, a child is a blessing, a gift from God. How many parents tragically forget that their children are blessings? Too many to mention. They could be experiencing the joy of watching a child blossom through nurturing and praise. Instead, they settle for impatience and disappointment in how their kids "turn out."

The same applies to the workplace. Most employees are important team players that bring energy, innovation and integrity to our businesses. Is appreciation for effort and acknowledgment of contributions reflected in the actions of their supervisors? Not nearly enough. Managers could be benefiting from the high productivity of a well-integrated team. Instead, they worry that things are not getting done and it will be their head that rolls as a result.

In order to connect to the world through Love, we must first correct our early perceptions which include negative judgment about ourselves. These counterproductive judgments began as we incurred "breaks" or impasses in our Spiritual Bridge. The correction is an inner process that requires mending the Spiritual Bridge through forgiveness: the relinquishment of judgment, followed by a thought of peace.

As you learn the skills of the five R's you will be taken through the steps for forgiveness. Each step brings you to a thought of peace and in so doing, empowers you to stay on the path of Love:

<u>RELINQUISHMENT of JUDGMENT</u>   <u>THOUGHT OF PEACE</u>

1. **Revealing the History:** *It happened.* ——— It was.
2. **Recognizing the Impasse:** *It is still happening.* ——— It is.
3. **Releasing the Past:** *I can exchange my purpose.* ——— I can.
4. **Responding to Fear:** *I know my purpose.* ——— I know.
5. **Reconnecting to the Spirit:** *I bridge to God in me.* — I Am.

Through the relinquishment of self judgment, we eliminate the obstacles to self knowledge. Notice at the midpoint, **Releasing the Past**, the thoughts transition into the powerful first person. We start out accepting that the "breaks" to the Bridge occurred and then advance to proclaiming our own inherent ability to mend the gap. We can go beyond being "in recovery" to being "recovered." Also notice how uncomplicated is a thought of peace. Its simplicity restores us to the innocence of the Spiritual Self.

Emotional recovery is greatly accelerated and quickly stimulated when you can go directly to the spiritual perspective. Astute psychotherapy is a healing relationship. It corrects our perception through the elimination of self-judgment and restores us to the **I Am**. Humans can then co-create spiritual alliances in every aspect of their lives: in their primary relationships, in their parenting, in the workplace, with friends, with "strangers."

Spiritual alliances are extremely powerful because when people are connected spirit-to-spirit, they increase the dynamics of faith in love, creativity, courage, confidence, trust and hope.

3

REVEALING THE HISTORY

My grievances hide the Light in me.

It was.

Why do we study history? I frequently ask this question during my seminars and invariably, the answer is twofold: 1) So that we have a better understanding of where we are today; and 2) So that we don't repeat the same mistakes. The way in which the world has evolved is of vital interest to people. They study it, read about it and watch it recreated in film and on TV. Clearly, we are deeply interested in history. The survivors of the Holocaust frequently plead with the world never to forget the genocide of Hitler, that it may never be repeated.

You yourself have a very important and revealing personal history called childhood. Have you ever taken the time to seriously consider it … to study it? Many of us have forgotten much of the past or perhaps have developed a selective recall about it. I'm not suggesting that you get bogged down in the past—far from it. You only need to review it as an opportunity to use it as a catalyst to make positive changes in the *here and now*. Your past was not all bad. The good stuff is not our concern right now. What we are interested in is how your judgment or perception of some bad stuff may have helped you incur some breaks in your own **Spiritual Bridge**, thereby negatively affecting your belief system.

A child is considered "impressionable" because when he first enters the world, he is conceivably about one hundred percent spiritual self. He is in the **I Am**. He has very limited sense of the physical, emotional, and intellectual selves. As the infant begins to move through the oversized, scary world, the other three soon begin to develop. This, for the most part is as it is supposed to be, except when the development of the other three is at the sacrifice of the Spiritual Self which only knows innocence, goodness, and Love. The development of the physical, intellectual, and emotional selves at the sacrifice of the Spiritual Self is also called the *ego*. When the child develops an ego, he is converting to a fear-based way of thinking which is virtually opposed to the powerful spiritual component. He moves from **I Am** to I am afraid. This unconscious process happens to all of us. That's just the way it is.

> I was shopping one day at a popular department store, where I witnessed a heartbreaking occurrence. A woman in her early thirties was shopping for her mother, also there in a wheelchair. The two young children of the thirty year-old woman, about three and four years old respectively, were present as well. The disabled mother was uncooperative, unpleasant, and displeased with whatever her daughter pulled from the racks as possibilities for purchase. As the first two generations continued along in this apparent exercise in futility, the third generation of little ones began to run around the department in a game of tag: in and out of the racks of clothes, giggling and having a great time.
>
> Their mother, frustrated with her own mother, began to target her annoyance at her offspring: threatening them with a beating if they didn't immediately call a halt to their game. The small children certainly tried to slow down, but it sure is hard for spirited children to harness what comes naturally. It seemed as if only seconds had elapsed before the mother of the youngsters dropped an armful of clothes and followed through on her promise and ran after the children. She grabbed hold of the little girl and began to beat on her unmercifully. I walked straight to the courtesy phone and summoned up the security guard. The disabled mother witnessed the call, wheeled over to her daughter and apprised her of the situation. The beating stopped with the concluding threat: "Just wait till I get you home!"

> The little girl collapsed to the floor, sucking her thumb and sobbing deeply. The guard came up shortly thereafter and looked on from a short distance away. After a few minutes, he left. What had occurred before my eyes was the transgenerational breaking of spirits. The disabled, "broken" mother was unconsciously breaking the Spiritual Bridge of her daughter, who in turn was breaking the Spiritual Bridge of her own little one. As the little girl sobbed, she was in the midst of retreating into a fear-based ego, separating from her Spiritual Self. It was a human tragedy in the making.

Fear-based behaviors are frequently handed down from generation to generation. Certain behavioral patterns become family styles that persist over time. I am sure some of you might have heard, "You're just like your father" or "Stop acting like your mother." It makes sense that we would act like our parents because they were our primary role models when we were young and our brains were developing! It doesn't matter who you take after, you are the ultimate decision maker of who you are.

Remember this formula: **EGO equals YOU minus YOUR SPIRITUAL PERSPECTVE**. Certain frightening, childhood experiences do their greatest harm on a spiritual level, because essentially that is all there is to be injured within the psyche of a child. So the child begins to separate from the most powerful part of his personality quite early. I use the adjective "powerful" in that the Spirit is completely love-based, the source of faith in oneself, hope, trust, and courage.

So let's take a trip down memory lane and closely look at where you have been. You've been in your Mother's womb, in her arms and in the arms of others. You were really small when the rest of the world seemed really big and many things were perceived by your little eyes as being much larger than life. You have probably forgotten about all that over the years. To quickly remember, simply take a second, put the book down and squat down close to the floor and look all around you. Quite a different perspective, wouldn't you say? Have you ever visited an elementary school classroom utilized by kindergarten or first grade? The chairs and desks are so tiny, so close to the floor. The world looks quite oversized and exaggerated through the eyes of a small child. The darkness looks very dark, an adult looks like a giant and a loud sound can be very startling.

You perceived early that certain things, certain people, certain places were big and scary and you didn't like that feeling of fear, so you buried it. A child automatically does this as a survival mechanism. After all, how can a defenseless child survive in a scary world? She can't. So in order to keep away from the feeling of fear, you began to develop certain **acting-in** or **acting-out** behaviors as a way to *distract* yourself from the unpleasant feeling.

You might have sucked your thumb, had nightmares, or wet the bed. Perhaps you had temper tantrums, you were painfully shy, or you were aggressive with other children. Maybe you did poorly in school or not as well as you might have. Maybe you got sick a lot. Conceivably you were too competitive or not competitive enough. These behaviors served as distractions from the unpleasant feeling of fear. Take a minute and remember some of your childhood traits and behaviors. They were the seedlings of traits and behaviors you possess today. Some of them are great. Some are huge obstacles in the way of you remembering who you really are.

An understanding of how they evolved empowers you in the present to decide which were useful and which were not. Maybe your parents didn't realize you were scared. They may have reacted to your acting-in or acting-out behaviors inappropriately. *It wasn't their fault.* They themselves were operating at a lack of knowledge and against the recognition of their own childhood fears. Many parents become very focused on the child's **acting-in** or **acting-out** as though that were the real problem when, in fact, it is really the child's solution to feeling afraid. Our parents were operating with very few psychological tools and historically many of us were parented basically the same way our parents were parented. For the most part, our parents reared us based on the information they got from their own parents. A lot of it was great; some of it was counterproductive.

After all, the entire field of psychology is reasonably new. Preceding generations did not have the knowledge that is available to us today. Also, the pioneering field of neuroscience is just beginning to understand how different neurocircuitries and neural pathways are formed to result in certain feeling states and behaviors (Begley, 2007). It is being acknowledged in recent times that the emotional lessons of a child actually sculpt the brain's circuitry and set the blueprint for future behaviors (Goleman, 1995). There is still so much more for us to learn.

There are those who appear on the surface to be more separated from their Spiritual Selves than others. The depth of the *impasse* or the break in the Spiritual Bridge depends on the intensity of the historical fear the child was initially subject to. What you will come to understand is that no matter how wide the gap, reconnecting is equally easy for everyone. You simply need to acknowledge that the break did, in fact, occur and then make the personal commitment to reconnect.

> Vincent came to me when he was forty-eight years old. He was constantly raging at his wife because she was disinterested in him sexually. No wonder, he was morbidly obese at 425 pounds. He wasn't overweight at the time they were married. At that time, he was fresh out of an inpatient weight-loss program and down almost 200 pounds. They married after a whirlwind courtship of three months and soon thereafter, Vincent began to regain the weight at a breakneck speed.
>
> Vincent shared with me during our first meeting that his mother was a severely battered wife who did virtually nothing about her intolerable marital situation. Vincent consciously remembered his mother fondling his genitals as early as three years old. This went on until puberty, when his mother than had Vincent perform intercourse with her. Father worked a night job and soon after he left for the evening, Mother called Vincent into her bedroom.
>
> Vincent began overeating as an acting-in distraction from the pain. Vincent carried enormous shame and anger about this experience: the key word being enormous, as his weight reflected. He also battled with extreme confusion about healthy adult sexuality. He was afraid, believed he was inadequate, and set up sexual protection by way of his obesity. I Am deteriorated into I am afraid and alone. His

> perception of the shocking early experience automatically cast an incestuous climate in his marriage. While Vincent was desperate to be physically intimate, the very idea of sex triggered the original shame and rage. Once those feelings were triggered, Vincent would binge-eat as a distraction from the unpleasantness of it all. His ever increasing size perpetuated the fear and shame. He soon got into the acting-out distraction of blaming his wife for their sexual troubles. Round and round went Vincent, until he identified the historical break and began to redefine his experience as an impasse in his Spiritual Bridge.
>
> Once he made the personal commitment to reconnect, he was empowered to correct his perception of the early abuse. Vincent changed the nature of his relationship with food and with women. Vincent started to enjoy his life.

Binge-eating is a very popular acting-in distraction, as evidenced by the obesity problem in America. Many children are given food when they are feeling upset, rather than be given the option of experiencing the upset until they are finished. People who binge-eat have chosen food as their distraction from painful feelings as they literally swallow down their fear and sadness that may very well have roots in an earlier time of their lives. Furthermore, they buffer themselves from attaching to others because of their large size. Ironically, many obese people report feelings of loneliness and isolation. It is important to remember that an eating disorder is only one type of distraction. There are a plethora of them. How do you distract yourself from feeling afraid?

Unfortunately, too many of us remain unaware of the unconscious reaction to fear. That's why you are reading this book: to become consciously aware of that which is unconsciously going on, as a form of empowerment. When we are in a place where an early fear is triggered, it is torture. The tendency is not unlike the predicament of Superman. Superman was all powerful, as long as he was out of the range of kryptonite. If kryptonite was close by, he could still be okay as long as it was enclosed in lead. Our early fears are the emotional kryptonite. The acting-in and acting-out distractions are the lead box. We operate powerfully until some external event occurs that flips the lid open on the lead box. Then watch out! We feel threatened and paralyzed.

Now some of you may be saying, "This is hopeless. How could one ever overcome a lifespan based on the repression of unconscious fear?" Don't worry. That feeling of hopelessness is a great indicator of your own personal separation. Remember that hope is a spiritually based behavior. It is easy to get back to hopefulness. The intensity of the negative historical experience is actually irrelevant. An historical experience is a memory and nothing more. It lurks around in the recesses of our mind. It simply does not exist in the present.

The particular meaning any memory has is the meaning we choose to ascribe to it. We can change the meaning at any time. You'll have to decide when you are ready to change the meaning of a memory. Perceiving a painful past experience in terms of a spiritual break motivates us to change its impact. Once you have come to understand and accept that the separation from the Spiritual Self did take place, reconnecting is similarly restorative for everyone. Operating from the spiritual perspective of Love, rather than the ego perspective of fear, restores us to our original **I Am** and places the painful past into the position of nothing more than a meaningless thought.

As the ego develops, through some very complicated neurocircuitry, as a way to repress the fear, the child becomes more and more separated from his spirit and grows with increasing difficulty in operating from a Love-based position. The acting-in and acting-out behaviors get more perplexing: aggression, intolerance, passivity, perfectionism, depression, isolation, anxiety, physical illness, etc. As this goes on, so does the growth of feelings of shame or inadequacy because the child, drawing judgment from the environment, basically believes he has difficulty functioning in a scary world. Remember that significant adults in our lives tended to converge on our *childhood distractions* from fear, rather than address fear directly. Judging the behavior of others, as an adult, is a popular acting-out which serves the one who is judging as a vehicle to stay dissociated from their own fear.

An eight-year-old girl, Tara, was brought in by her mother to begin working with me. The girl had been diagnosed with rheumatoid arthritis six months earlier and Mother claimed Tara was also exhibiting signs of depression. Mother was a warm, outgoing person who was in a deep state of pity for her youngest daughter.

As I spoke privately with Tara, she verbalized her frustration at Mother's consistent limit-setting on Tara's life. She prohibited Tara from many physical activities, insisted that she rest in bed for prolonged periods of time, and continually told the child that she wasn't looking very well.

Tara was in a state where insult was being added to injury. She lost sight of I Am and was repeating to herself "I am sick and disabled." She really wanted to overcome her disease, at the very least on an emotional level, but Mother's continued ruminating was making it increasingly difficult for her to do so. Tara was feeling poor in spirit and was beginning to believe that her disease was very scary because it rendered her incapable of functioning in the world. Perhaps Mother 'needed' Tara's illness as a distraction from her own feelings of fear and inadequacy.

I asked Tara to take a seat in the waiting room and send Mother in. I began asking Mother some questions about her marriage. She started off impatiently telling me that it was just great and demanded to know what all this had to do with Tara's awful set of circumstances. I responded by stating that it had everything to do with it and continued asking questions. In about five minutes, the tale was told. Mother revealed that she thought her husband was a womanizer and she was terrified to address the issue with him because she believed he would opt to leave her rather than work it out.

When Mother was seven years old, her father abandoned the family to take up with another woman. Back then, this was considered to be far too shameful a topic for open discussion, much less resolution. Yet, this significant historical event was very powerful in its unacknowledged

> state. Paternal abandonment is a sure break in the Spiritual Bridge, where a child might easily grow up with issues of betrayal, mistrust, and self blame.
>
> Tara's illness presented a perfect opportunity for Mother to set up a distraction of pity in order to avoid her own historical feelings of fear and inadequacy that had nothing to do with Tara at all. I never saw Tara in treatment again. Not coincidentally, when Mother began couple counseling with her husband, Tara began to rapidly improve and refused to let her illness be the excuse for not enjoying a quality life.

The family system dynamic of triangulation is illustrated in this example. Triangulating families tend to focus all their attention on the behavior or well being of a particular child. By doing this, they distract themselves from some significant ongoing, unresolved marital conflict (Titleman, 1998). Sometimes the triangulation strategy does not appear to be a negative thing on the surface. For example, there are some couples who distract themselves from necessary conflict by having a child enrolled in a overabundance of activities, which takes up enormous spans of time for the parents. Sometimes the couple is distracted by a very rebellious child who takes up all their emotional time with constant worry. While there are many different scenarios or distractions within families, they can be simplified down to a fear-based need to circumvent a more pressing issue.

A more simplistic example is provided by a personal historical experience of my own. As a child of about five or six, I was chubby with very thick, very curly hair that sort of had a mind of its own. Now at three or four, these traits were considered by other grown-ups to be adorable. Wow! Was I in for a shock when I started kindergarten and my peers teased and demeaned me about these very same traits.

Now you may be saying from your adult perspective, "So big deal. Who wasn't teased by other kids?" True enough, from the mature point of view. In fact, my parents, in their pragmatic adulthood, unwittingly minimized my pain by giving me feedback such as, "Just ignore it" or "Stop acting like a baby." Sometimes they'd throw me a cliché like "Sticks and stones can break your bones, but words will never hurt you." However, from my little five year-old perspective, it was a very big deal and words certainly *did* hurt me. This is another example of adding insult to injury. There I was terrified to go to school and experience more taunting and at home I was getting messages that I was incompetent at functioning in the world because I was in pain.

Now let me make it clear that I am *not* blaming my parents. Their intent was to help and they were uncomfortable with my personal expression of pain because it brought them too close to their own, which they were busy distracting themselves from. While I continued to go on from the unpleasant experience, the break to my Spiritual Bridge remained until many years later, when I finally decided to stop distracting myself from it and give myself permission to have my woe and then let it go through forgiveness.

Until I acknowledged the presence of that particular break, it remained an obstacle. How can you mend a tear if you refuse to notice it's there? How was it an obstacle? From that break to my Spiritual Bridge, I retreated into my ego and began to believe that I wasn't very attractive and I began to feel afraid of rejection. **I Am** became "I am ugly and I am unacceptable".

As I moved on from the original upset in kindergarten, I found myself never being popular throughout my school career, I was the last one picked for teams, I had very few dates, I basically felt isolated, and I took few risks in the social arena. My grades were always perfect … probably a compensation for what I was sorely missing. Finally, I found myself in a new high school in eleventh grade where I was basically ignored through graduation. The impact of the original scary experience went on from there until I was in my twenties. Incidentally, until then, I wore my hair short and controlled. Since I corrected my perception of the original experience, I have a bit of a reputation for my **big** hair and I wear it any way that suits my desire.

Your personal history is so important because it is where you began to make judgment about yourself and your place in the world as you moved through those early experiences. It was the decision making place for what have become the objects of your faith—for what you believe, and for what you have unconsciously set up and lived out through the course of your life.

As a child encounters scary situations and scary people, he begins to incur breaks in the Spiritual Bridge, obstructing a clear neural pathway to the Higher Mind. The common historical events that result in spiritual breaks are those that personify themes of betrayal and abandonment. As a result, the child begins to operate from his ego, caught in a fear-based perspective that he will be at risk to perpetuate and re-create. As an adult, he deserves to make the conscious and personal commitment to correct his original perception, remember his Higher Mind, and let his spiritual perspective be his guide.

4

RECOGNIZING THE IMPASSE

Forgive yourself and forget all senseless journeys and all goal-less aims. They have no meaning. You cannot escape from what you are.

It is.

History repeats itself. I can remember many times as a child when I swore to myself that I would never say to my own children some of the inane things my mother said to me. I humble myself before you now as I confess to the number of times I have nearly had to gag myself in order not to say to my kids **exactly** what she said to me! Similarly, those of us who have unresolved fear about the past are doomed to repeat it. We repeat it in our primary "relationships", in our parenting, in the workplace, and in our friendships. The tendency to do this is unconscious, yet so seductive and addictive; we will actually attract personality types into our experiences that are easy targets for the projection of our childhood fears (Hendrix, 1990).

The acting-in or acting-out distractions of our childhood have "matured" at this point. A thumb sucker may develop into an alcohol/drug abuser. A painfully shy child may develop into a depressed adult. A little more sophisticated, but distractions all the same, we re-create the past with the help of our distractions. Once the history has been revealed, we are able to get conscious about or *recognize* how we set up the impasse again and again in adulthood.

Katherine, a thirty-six year-old reservations clerk for a posh hotel, came to see me when she was three months pregnant with her fourth child. Her first three children were fathered by a man she had divorced two years prior to our first meeting. The current pregnancy was the result of an extended relationship she was having with a very noncommittal man. Katherine claimed she was on the Pill at the time of conception. Katherine was the third child of an alcoholic blue collar worker who had been diagnosed as paranoid schizophrenic. He had been abandoned by his own mother as a child and left in the hands of an extremely violent father. Thus, he hated women and believed they could not be trusted.

Katherine's older siblings were brutalized by this man. She was a change-of-life baby, conceived shortly after her father was released from an eight-month stay in a private psychiatric hospital. While she was rarely physically abused as a child, Her father would covertly sexually abuse her by repeatedly calling her horrific names such like: "whore, slut, and fucking cunt". Her mother would object, but due to complicated circumstances, never offered protection by escaping with her daughter from these sessions of verbal abuse.

After two abortions, Katherine married her long-term boyfriend at the age of nineteen years. Seven years into the marriage, she found out her husband was an active sex addict and finally filed for divorce when it became apparent that he was not motivated for recovery. Before her divorce was final, she took up with an older man, Russ, who owned a number of small nursing homes. He was extremely attentive and ever-present early in their relationship, but soon became less and less interested. Katherine found out, in fact, that he was sleeping with several other women while he continued to be with her ... another sex addict.

The more unavailable Russ became, the more Katherine aggressively went after him. It turns out this pregnancy was her last futile attempt to have him. It didn't work. Russ himself was the child of divorced parents. His rageful, embittered mother made it impossible for Father to visit with the children. As a result, Russ was kidnapped back and forth between parents throughout his childhood and forced to live all over the country as a hostage and a fugitive. Russ blamed his mother for the horror of his experience. He despised women as an adult. Therefore, he distracted himself from his historical fear of abandonment through the acting-out behavior of sexual addiction, where he displaced his maternal rage onto the objectification of women.

Russ came to see me only a few times. During our last visit he threatened to steal the coming male baby and take off for Costa Rica if Katherine didn't get off his back! This return to the kidnapping scenarios of his youth was not a union of spirits. This was a "relationship" built upon collaboration in fear, which makes it no relationship at all. Katherine was busy re-creating her paternal abandonment by collaborating with men who hated and dehumanized women. Russ was actively reliving his own past through reproducing with an angry woman, who he perceived as untrustworthy. They could potentially collaborate this way for years and pass the legacy down to the next generation.

Since we learn to connect to others through the early attachment styles we experienced in infancy and childhood, we are unconsciously wired to repeat these earlier styles in our ongoing relationships (Siegel, 1999). They can become patterns in our life and many times they can contribute to insecurities and dissatisfying relationships. This is a useful time to consider your attachment pattern. Your caregivers were the engineers of the way in which your early experiences influenced certain changes in your brain function and behaviors. Identifying your attachment pattern allows you the opportunity to identify your relationship style and decide to make a healthy shift. How do you make your attachments? If you don't make secure attachments, then you are using either an avoidant or an anxious style.

Collaborations in fear can be further explored by looking at Stephen Karpman's Drama Triangle. His Drama Triangle is drawn from Berne's

(1964) concept of Transactional Analysis. Visualize, if you will, a triangle with three different roles at each point. One role is the victim position, the next is the rescuer position, and the third is the perpetrator position. When we are stuck in a fear-based perspective, we interact with others by moving around this drama triangle, continually interchanging the roles.

DRAMA TRIANGLE

victim

rescuer   perpetrator

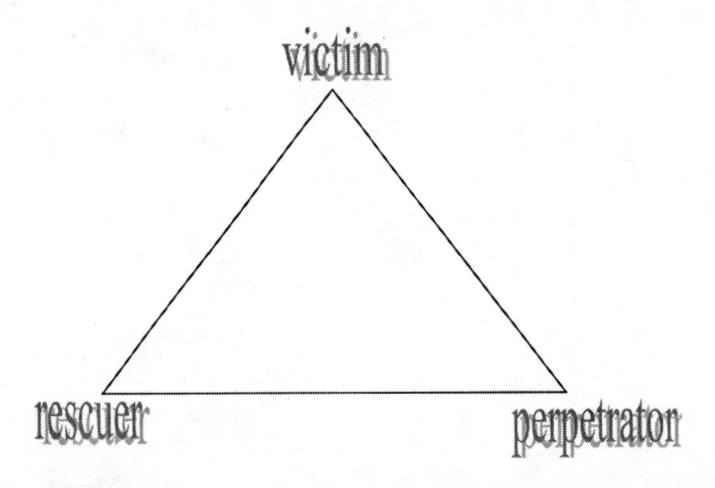

> A medical doctor, James, came to see me because he was having marital problems. There were problems all along in the four years he was with Christa, but things had really escalated when she looked on his computer and found that he had quite a collection of pornographic pictures. Christa confronted James and told him to get some help or she was filing for divorce. James wasn't very enthused about working with me at first because he felt like he was being bullied into seeking help. I pointed out to him that he was a very bright man and he certainly knew that he would be caught when his wife looked on his computer. I interpreted the acting-out as a clear cry for some help. James felt relieved when it was put that way and he began to talk.

James was very unhappy in his marriage. He was a quiet, gentle kind of guy who tended to keep to himself. Of course, the more he kept to himself, the more Christa came after him. She was angry, sad, and complained to him that she did not receive enough love, affection, or intimacy. James complained to me that he could never get close to Christa because she was ill and never wanted to have sex. She would have one malady after another: sinus infections, fibromyalgia, heart palpitations, flu, colds. Christa came from a family where the women made career a priority. She was intelligent, achieved several masters' degrees, yet never found a job that seemed to meet her needs. Christa struggled with a sense of inadequacy about her vocational ambivalence.

James felt put upon by Christa to take responsibility for her health. She was constantly asking him for medical advice. He resented it, but being a doctor what did he expect? James didn't like the system, but abdicated his power. He distracted himself by becoming depressed with every missed opportunity to state his position. He chose a more covert way to tell his wife what he thought. His attempt to get her attention worked. They traveled the Drama Triangle, interchanging the roles. James was the victim who rarely had his needs met and still endured verbal attacks from Christa, the perpetrator. James was the rescuer who diagnosed and advised his wife. James was the perpetrator who through his passive-aggressive act, behaved abusively to his wife. Christa was the victim who was frequently ill. She was the rescuer in assuming the managerial role in the relationship. She was the perpetrator in her pointed verbal attacks on James. James was weary with this fear-based system. He wanted to face the challenge of a real marriage.

Revealing the history really helped us to get a handle on the situation. James was the last born, only male in a family of three children. His mother was an "invalid" who was chronically sick, in bed most of the time and very powerful in her supine position. To this day, no one is certain about exactly what is wrong with her. His father dedicated his entire life to nursing the woman and her poor health set the tone for how the family system would evolve. The children were expected to keep quiet and take care of themselves lest their mother have a setback. His father had no needs in the marriage because it would be absurd to expect anything from a partner who was unable to function. James recalled feeling cheated and ignored as a child. He had no relationship with his mother and was more of a parent to his father in being cooperative with his father's need to play nurse.

James had recreated the impasse on several levels. Choosing a career of doctor only seems logical after we reveal the history. Attracting himself to a sickly woman from who little could be expected also makes sense. The choice to keep quiet and ask for nothing also fits in to the re-creation. His acting-in distraction of depression and his acting-out distraction of pornography helped keep James dissociated from some very painful feelings. Feelings he had postponed having for many years.

James did not give much consideration to a personal sense of God and he reported doing nothing in the way of nurturing his Spiritual Self. That didn't surprise me. You can't nurture something to which you are not connected. Maternal abandonment, no matter what form it takes, is a severe break to the Spiritual Bridge. James went from I Am to I am a victim and I am unworthy. James could not trust women and he had no faith in healthy love. He did not have the courage to state his position and ask to have his needs met, and last but not least, he was prohibiting himself from accessing forgiveness because he had not yet acknowledged his anger, sadness and shame. The Drama Triangle helped sustain the original break, until James recognized how the impasse was repeated in his adult life. James looked calm and happy, but behind the gentle exterior was a very angry and sad man.

Many of us were raised in codependent families of origin. We watched one parent caretaking or managing the other (Beattie, 1986). The messages that get hard-wired into the developing brain of a child in that type of family system is that managing or controlling the other is more important than staying clear and centered in oneself. The sad part is that every time a person manages or controls the other, they have accidentally denied the other an important opportunity to manage her/himself. We see this in alcoholic/addictive families, where the spouse of the addict manages the addict. We also see it in domestic abuse where the spouse of an abuser manages the mood of the abuser, rather than support him/her in controlling one's own temper. Furthermore, if we were raised in a family that used codependent approaches, these attachment styles become our impasse and we unconsciously repeat these patterns in our adult relationships.

This brings us squarely to "victimhood." Beware the temptation to be a victim! Victims are not expected to be accountable or responsible. The victim position may seem like the easy way out of internal and/or external conflict. But the so-called easy way, quickly becomes the hard way, when one realizes that victims are also perceived as helpless and powerless to take control over the quality of their lives. This perceived helplessness attracts to the victim exactly what he does not need, a perpetrator or a rescuer. The behaviors of someone stuck in the victim position are eventually hostilely perceived by the person on the receiving end. People who are separated from the Spiritual Self and who operate from fear instead of love tend to see themselves as victims. Consequentially, they actuate themselves into the other roles of rescuer and perpetrator without conscious awareness. If you see yourself as a victim, then you are actually recognizing yourself as the victim of your *original* break in the Spiritual Bridge. You are probably re-enacting early breaks in your present experience. Recognizing the impasse when it is triggered empowers you to mend the gap at any time you choose.

Once we *recognize the impasse*, as we set it up in the present, we also notice that we basically move around in a constant state of separation anxiety. Traditionally, separation anxiety is a term that refers to the upset a child feels when he must detach from a parent. I believe that *all* anxiety is actually separation anxiety. I define separation anxiety as the chronic underlying distress we feel as a result of being separated from the most loving and nurturing **spiritual** part of *ourselve*s. This sensitivity is as unpleasant in adulthood as it was in childhood and we stick to certain distractions as a way to avoid feeling it. Separation anxiety would keep us trapped inside the Drama Triangle, a fear-based system. Recognizing and meeting this anxiety enables us to get out of the triangle altogether.

> Bill was suffering from deep depression. He came to see me shortly after being fired from his job at a bank and divorced from his wife of three years. Bill, at the usually energetic age of twenty-eight, was lethargic and lifeless. He was very physically attractive and extremely articulate. He was the sort of guy who appears to have everything going for him. But, Bill didn't see it that way. He had been raised in a family that included an alcoholic father, who mysteriously lost his job as a commercial airline pilot and then went into auto mechanics, and a mother who simply put up with his father's constant drinking when she wasn't imbibing herself. Everyone obeyed the **No-Talk Rule**, so the alcohol problem was never discussed. Bill had a younger sister who was very overweight.
>
> While growing up, Bill was a target for his father's profound sense of his own inadequacy and incompetence. He criticized Bill for just about everything he did. One scene from his youth that Bill recounted many times in-session was when his father demanded Bill, ten years old at the time, mow the lawn. Bill set about the task, feeling pretty clear on what he needed to do to get the thing mowed. His father flew outside in a drunken rage, grabbed the mower from Bill, yelling at him that he couldn't do anything right and if he wasn't going to do things right, then don't do them at all! There was a clear break to the Spirit.
>
> Bill banked that incident and unintentionally began to re-create it again and again in his adult life. He couldn't do marriage, he couldn't do his job at the bank, and, shortly after he started therapy, he sabotaged another job as a customer service rep with an airline, by

being chronically late. He burned up the engine in his pick-up because he never checked or changed the oil. His parents had to buy him a new one and shamed him about it all the way to the Motor Vehicle Bureau. When he was demoted to a baggage handler because of poor work performance, I put my therapeutic foot down.

I explained to Bill that he was ready to recognize the impasse. His resistance to do so felt like a set up for his therapy to join the ranks as one more failure. I was not available to take part in that, not even as an observer. I pointed out his unconscious set-up of his life so that he repeatedly landed back on his father's doorstep to be rescued financially. I interpreted for Bill how he carried his father's own feelings of worthlessness and how he inadvertently helped maintain the alcoholic system by certainly providing a great source of distraction for his parents. Bill felt abandoned by his parents, but he maintained an unhealthy attachment to them by collaborating in fear. Children who perceive abandonment by their parents will usually devise some unhealthy way to stay attached. If Bill didn't remain attached to his parents through fear and shame, maybe there would be no attachment at all. Ironically, every time he collaborated with them in fear and shame, he ended up being emotionally abandoned again. Whenever Mom and Dad rescued him, they berated him for his irresponsibility.

Once Bill recognized, this, he realized that he couldn't lose what he never had. Bill had to learn to be a different sort of father to himself than the one he had historically experienced. He began to be more responsible at his job, he got another one at night, he got his own apartment, and he started to date. Bill began to mend the gap in his Spiritual Bridge through forgiveness of himself and others and in so doing, he could better access the powerful dynamics generated by the Spiritual Self: creativity, courage, confidence, trust in himself, faith in his abilities and hope for the future.

Recognizing the impasse can be achieved by examining some of the underlying and unspoken themes in our families of origin. Many times these themes were subtle and temperate in their orientation. For example, in some families boys are treated disproportionately more important than girls. In other families, religion and religious practices crowded out healthy and direct communication. Money issues, conflicting values, family secrets can all contribute. In other situations, how the family was perceived by the outside world was more important than what was truly happening within the system. In recognizing the impasse, don't always look for the obvious. Many times it is the unspoken themes or codes of silence that drive the impasse forward, sometimes for generations. Identify some of the patterns in your family of origin that may have precipitated an impasse in your own personal spiritual bridge.

Those of us attached to the past are bound to unconsciously re-create it. We've been doing it for so long; we don't even notice it anymore. The pattern has developed into a physically powerful neurocircuitry in the brain (Schore, 2003). Once that path has imbedded itself into the gray matter, it becomes a freeway for neurons to travel. They automatically journey that well traveled road.

Attachment to the past also carries an addictive quality to it. The familiarity of being stuck there has a perverse sense of comfort simply because we are so connected to the associated unpleasant feeling states. *Recognizing* when we are replaying an updated version of a historical scene, and experiencing, rather than avoiding the separation anxiety that gets triggered in the replay, are some very important skills in mending the Spiritual Bridge.

Recognizing the Impasse is our wake-up call to do something different. Experiencing our separation anxiety motivates us to remember God in Us, the **I Am**. When we reconnect to the spiritual perspective, we realize that we are never abandoned and therefore, never alone.

5

RELEASING THE PAST

I give you to the Higher Mind as part of myself. In the name of my freedom, I choose your release because I recognize we will be released together.

I Can.

Our attachment to the past bars our bridging to the Spiritual Self. This Self is an inner consciousness that stays peacefully centered in the here and now. Having, to this point, determined an impasse and decided to no longer retreat from it, we can now begin to mend the break in our Spiritual Bridge. This is experienced as a challenge because we are in the throws of separation anxiety at the time we call upon ourselves to begin the repair. Traditional Psychology would coin this as "free floating anxiety". It *is* free floating in that as we let go of our false idols we fear drifting off into oblivion due to disconnection. We can now take a leap of faith that in letting go, we give ourselves back to our personal concept of God and never need be a victim of anxiety again.

When we release the past, we release ourselves to exchange our purpose. As we give fear to our personal God, we receive our God in ourselves. When we exchange our purpose, we change our mind from *separation through fear* to *connection through our* **Higher Mind**. We begin the transition from "I am alone" to **I Am**. We transform the objects of our faith, by no longer inspiring the painful past. Unpleasant feeling states and counterproductive behaviors are no longer the altar at which we choose to worship. Instead, the Higher Mind or **Love** is where we extend ourselves to keep vigil. The First Commandment: "Worship no god but Me.", begins to make perfect sense.

What exactly *is* the past? Webster's dictionary gives: "the time before or time gone by". What does *that* mean? The past is a span of time. Is it tangible? I don't think so. Our memories of time gone by are all that really exist and they exist only in our minds. Memories are not really the past per se; they are only perceptions of it. It is important to realize that what we remember is far less impacting than how we remember it. The historical action is over. It is only our judgment of it that actually remains.

A mother's memory of a nuclear family may very different from her child's. Mother may perceive it to have been wonderful and her role as mother to have been very positive and helpful. The child's perception may be different. The child may have perceived it to have been at times, unsafe. Perhaps, when Mother was angry, she was perceived by her child as a scary woman. Now, who was right and who was wrong? Neither, yet both family members! When a child decides to release the past, she/he understands that the memory of Mom's behavior was one individual's perspective. When a child exchanges her/his purpose from *fear* to **Love**, the self judgment that in light of the memory, she/he was unworthy of receiving love is relinquished.

The point is that a perception of the past exists in our minds and that is all there is left of it. The events themselves are much less meaningful than how you took in the events as they occurred. How you took them in: experienced them, processed them and judged yourself in their context; is what makes up your perception of them. You can change your perception any time you choose to relinquish judgment. When you change your perception of the past, you have released it.

Now I realize there are many of you who use your perceptions of the past as the objects of your faith and I can hear the balking: "Right, Ellie. My father beat me to a pulp with his belt and I have a faulty perception of it!" Yes, your Father **did** beat you with a belt and it appears he's still doing it, only now he has your permission to do so. You see, the beating itself no longer exists. The beating hurt you physically at the time it happened. It was very painful.

Today, only your perception of it remains. It is important to grasp that the beating itself never had any meaning. The way you *felt,* emotionally at the time it happened imparts the only meaning the beating has. How did you feel when you were being beaten? Scared, sad, angry, shameful are words which probably describe your feelings. What have you done about those feelings? Perhaps you have distracted yourself through some acting-in or out behavior. You may even now take that painful perception of the past and project it onto people and circumstances today in a counterproductive fashion. Those negative feelings are still there and because you don't attend to them, you are stuck with a perception of the past that undoubtedly gets played out again and again in the here and now. So your father still metaphorically beats on you, only now he has your permission to do so.

Such complicity is not the healthy, healing way to deal with a painful history. Although some might believe that personality becomes fixed through early childhood experiences, it is very clear from recent research that through training your mind, you can beneficially alter the structure of your brain to achieve a better feeling outcome (Begley, 2007)! You do not have to be a prisoner of the past!

> A young woman named Nora came to see me because she was having ongoing conflict with her boyfriend. She found herself reacting to hateful remarks he repeatedly made about gay people. She stated that she felt afraid and offended by these remarks and even though she had communicated this to her boyfriend, he continued the verbal assault. I asked a few questions about his upbringing, feeling certain it would shed some light on his homophobic behavior. Sure enough, the young man had been subjected to some very hateful disciplinary techniques at the hands of his stepfather when he was a boy.
>
> Once, when he was about six years old, he went crying to his stepfather because his younger sister had grabbed a doll away from him. The stepfather became enraged and called the little boy a "sissy". He then forced the child to wear a dress to school every day for a week.

> Need I explain more? The boy must have felt so frightened and ashamed to be wearing a dress and so distressed about any feminine traits he possessed, that he eventually distracted himself from the continuing shame by projecting it outward as prejudice.
>
> Sadly, from a spiritual perspective, any attack on someone else is equivalent to an attack on oneself. Every time this young man attacked gays, he was ultimately attacking himself for his own healthy feminine side, thereby digging himself deeper and deeper into a fear-based perspective. The fear Nora felt about all this was largely an experience of the very fear from which her boyfriend had so viciously distracted himself. Eventually, Nora broke up with him.
>
> The boyfriend's father had no doubt believed he was teaching the child a valuable social lesson. His child took in the experience quite differently. The adult child is now faced with a truth that is no longer about his father; it is completely about himself and his perception of his father. His father was obviously homophobic and now the adult child has re-created and perpetuated the same prejudice a generation later … a re-enacted hatred which, in fact, cost him a loving heterosexual relationship.

Some people have a sense of identity that is built upon what their caregivers told them about themselves. If someone was repeatedly told as a child that they were stupid, or clumsy, or ugly, or a sissy, or a tomboy, or the greatest, or the best, or the smartest, those remarks become a basis of self identity that sometimes get in the way of the person exploring and discovering who he or she really is for him/herself (O'Hanlon, 1999). We deserve to create our own identities.

Recognizing, to any degree, the involvement of our parents in early spiritual breaks tempts us to blame our parents. This fixes us firmly in a relentless Drama Triangle. We identify ourselves as victims and believe that unless our parents fix it or apologize, we are forever at the mercy of their crimes. We are powerless and feel out of control. It's actually not about your parents anymore. Now it is all about you and your perceptions of them. Continuing to blame or judge parents, or anyone else for that matter, is just a way to distract yourself from your own spiritual separation anxiety, fear is truly the object of your faith. Through judging your parents, you judge yourself as unworthy of bridging to your God in you.

How do we change our fearful perception of the past, in order to release it and reconnect to our own powerful spiritual selves? Through forgiveness; that's how.

Forgiveness: **the relinquishment of judgment followed by a thought of peace**; is the binding material of the Spiritual Bridge. It is the stuff that keeps the bridge intact as a span to the Spiritual Self. Without forgiveness, there will always be an impasse in the Bridge, making it impossible to connect to our greatest Natural Resource. **Releasing the Past** requires the first step of forgiveness. **Responding to Fear** requires the second.

Forgiveness includes the correction of one's perception through the relinquishment of judgment. The events of the past are not the obstacle in letting go, it is our repeated decision to cast judgment on ourselves and the people connected to the events that detain us in it, sometimes for a lifetime. The choice to judge someone, as good or bad, right or wrong, starts with judging ourselves. When we are fearful and separated, we regrettably tend to scold ourselves.

> Kayleigh came to counseling because she was having difficulty shaking off a deep depression she reported having since the death of her first child, Todd, at the tender age of seventeen. He died from heart failure while attending school. He had two holes in his heart at birth. He was operated on at two years old to repair the holes and when the doctors started his heart back up, it would not beat on its own. They implanted a pacemaker which seemed to do the trick. Todd lived a "normal" life till he keeled over in class.
>
> Kayleigh shared in her first session that she was the first born to a very shaming, controlling mother. When Kayleigh entered into adolescence, Mom began to attack her regarding her behavior with boys. Rather than sit and have an informative talk about the birds and the

bees, she threatened Kayleigh about promiscuity and suggested to her daughter that she was provocative and "loose" with pubescent young men. Kayleigh finally embodied her mother's theme by becoming pregnant at sixteen years old. The young man involved with the pregnancy brought Kayleigh a "morning after pill" when she told him the news. He advised her that when she took the pill, she would begin to bleed and she would lose the pregnancy. Kayleigh was so terrified to be pregnant and judged as unworthy, she swallowed it. Nothing happened.

Kayleigh met someone on the beach a few weeks later. He married her and claimed the pregnancy as a result of their marriage. Todd was born with a major birth defect. Kayleigh blamed herself and when Todd died from a broken heart, she began a serious course of acting-in through her depression.

The first session I met with Kayleigh, she made comment about the unattractive placement of the furniture. Shortly thereafter, she remarked angrily that I was looking out the window. The second session, she began to pre-empt my feedback by saying things like, "Now Ellie, don't go saying any of that stupid 'You are a good person and you're okay' psycho-garbage to me!"

I took in a relaxing breath as I looked at her and responded, "Kayleigh, I wasn't going to say anything of the sort. I am having a reaction and I need to take a risk with you. My perception of some of your behaviors in building a relationship with me is that you are trying to connect to me in shame. Some judgmental remarks have tipped me off to this style. If you are being judgmental with me, then I imagine that you must be very judgmental with yourself. Perhaps this is a style you re create from your mother's role modeling."

Kayleigh settled into her chair. "Yes", she said, "I am just like her and I hate myself for it." I had a confused expression on my face as I remarked, "So, are you now judging yourself for being judgmental?" She laughed for the first time since we had met and its tone was melodious. "I sure am, aren't I?" Then we both laughed together as some healing was taking place.

We need to remember that our purpose on earth is certainly not to abuse ourselves. When we self abuse, we are competing against our God, rather than relating to Her/Him. <u>The Course in Miracles</u> (1975) states, "It is necessary for the student/teacher of God to realize, not that he should not judge, but that he can not. In giving up judgment, he is merely giving up what he did not have ...; he puts himself in a position where judgment through him, rather than by him can occur." Furthermore, when we operate from the spirit, we observe things from an inner consciousness that knows no separation. Therefore, one person's AIDS is everyone's; one person's grief is everyone's, one lie is a universal lie.

Forgiveness is for people, not for actions. When we are faced with an awful mistake, be it our own or someone else's, it would be far more effective to forgive ourselves and/or the other and give the mistake to the Higher Mind. The relinquishment of judgment invites wisdom in to handle the problem. Instead of the cliché, "God never gave me anything I can't handle", which keeps us in the victim position, we say, "I never gave myself or anyone else anything that God can't handle." When forgiveness is practiced in this manner, watch the course of events that follow work in a way to rectify the mistake. Holding onto judgment simply keeps breathing life into the mistake so that in our perception, it is happening over and over again.

Kayleigh was given a homework assignment. She was asked to meditate about the events of the past without any self judgment. As she practiced this, she realized that she was at an impasse in her Spiritual Bridge. She considered the past without feeling anything at all. She faced her Separation Anxiety, rather than retreat from it through depression. She took a leap of faith, exchanged her purpose from self abuse to connecting with Love, relinquished judgment and therefore, changed her mind. As Kayleigh became more centered on mending her Spiritual Bridge, her clinical symptoms diminished. She began to become more social and not coincidentally, she met a woman at work who shared that she too, had lost a child in a similar way. Kayleigh helped her friend bring the loss to closure through forgiveness and Love. Kayleigh also began strengthening her relationships with her two younger daughters, who really needed the unconditional love of an available mother. Kayleigh let herself heal and the effects extended out to heal the lives of others. Spiritual Bridging creates spiritual alliances.

When was the last time you forgave yourself? When was the last time you asked for forgiveness, remembering you are worthy of it. You probably haven't done any of these recently. And we all suffer, because unforgiving behaviors have made a world mentality which dictates: attack, be attacked, or avoid it all and take no risks.

Did you know you could be forgiven without formally saying you are sorry? Did you know that you can forgive someone who has never apologized to you? Nothing does my own heart more good than when I forgive myself for some acting-out distraction and tell my husband, "I've acted like such a jerk. Will you forgive me?" However there are certain mistakes gone by that I can no longer rectify in person. For these, I've chosen to forgive myself.

Forgiveness is a purely reciprocal process. When you forgive yourself, the other involved is forgiven as well. Every time you forgive yourself, you see the meaning in forgiving others. When you forgive others, you are no longer attached to them through underlying fear and shame. Collaborations in fear and shame precipitate more of the same and draw in a lot of negativity. These types of attachment grow to be avoidant or anxious and imprison us at the impasse. They prohibit us from realizing the power of the Spirit.

Justification is the obstacle to forgiveness. We think we have the right to bear a grievance based on our perceptions of the past. Our perceptions are points of view, not God's truth. Justification is the misuse of the intellectual self to set up an acting-in distraction from our fearful separation anxiety. We are so used to our pain and suffering, we practically worship them. If we were to give them up, we believe there would be a huge inner void. For some, the release of pain and suffering would throw us into such an identity crisis, we think there would be nothing left at all. So, in order to sustain a false sense of security, we unconsciously uphold fear as the object of our faith by justifying our reasons to be angry and to withhold forgiveness. We do this most frequently to ourselves, although we are largely unaware of it.

Whenever we are agitated at another, we are simultaneously scolding ourselves! The next time you feel very upset with someone else; take notice of how you are really judging yourself as unworthy of regard. Whenever I perceive my husband has not treated me well, it invariably indicates I am berating myself.

It is also important to understand that someone else's mistake never justifies our own behavioral choices. Every now and then I find myself in a traffic situation where someone chooses to feel angry about how I have handled my vehicle. They sometimes communicate their irritation by giving me a hateful gesture. I blow them a kiss in return. No one else is responsible for my thoughts, feelings and behaviors except me. I'd never want it to be any different because I choose to be in control of myself. Having someone else at my helm can be very distressing and downright dangerous.

> Annemarie came to see me shortly after she had an abortion. She was in major depression because although she didn't want to terminate her pregnancy, her fiancé insisted because he didn't want children. Her real problem was not the abortion. Her real problem was that she was collaborating with a man who was very wealthy, very powerful and very abusive. The two years Annemarie had spent with this man had taken her to depths of despair she never knew she could sink to. He was constantly denouncing her and she spent much of her time feeling shameful about some new piece of feedback he fed her, attesting to her inadequacy. He rarely bought her anything and they never went anywhere. He insisted she shower before sex, he insisted on anal sex, even though it was not her cup of tea and he always showered after sex. He criticized her social skills, her cooking and her decorating taste. Her teeth weren't good enough, her breasts weren't big enough, her skin wasn't clear enough.

She underwent a number of plastic surgeries trying to physically please him, but they were never acceptable, either. Annemarie was a bright, attractive young woman who held a vice presidential position for one of the town's major utilities, yet she perceived herself as a valueless piece of human sludge.

Annemarie's poor perception of herself began in the streets of the lower east side of New York. She was raised in a slum by immigrant parents who did not aspire to the American dream. Her father, who she described as a "bum," never worked because of a disability she believed existed only his mind. Her mother had to work many hours as a seamstress in a sweat shop to help raise her son and daughter. Her father was scary and unkind. He would rage at Annemarie's mother, as a distraction from his own shame, as soon as she entered the apartment after a long day's work. Her mother ignored his attacks.

Annemarie described herself looking like a street urchin as a child, going to school in cast-off rags that didn't match and attracted a lot of cruel remarks from the kids borne out of a tough neighborhood. Her father spent all his time down on the corner, playing cards with other unmotivated men. When Annemarie wasn't being taunted by the kids at school, she was alone upstairs in the apartment being terrorized by her older brother. She didn't have many possessions: only a dog and a doll that she adored.

One day her brother chased her around the apartment until he got hold of the doll and in one yank; he tore off its head and hurled it at Annemarie. Another day she went down to the market to pick up some food to start dinner and when she returned, her brother had taken her dog somewhere and left it, never to be seen again. Her brother hit her, screamed at her, and threatened her. Annemarie told her parents, but no one protected her.

The attacks went on for years. Annemarie saw herself as an unwanted child of God and grew up with a self concept that she was a bag lady. No matter how much money she made or how many nice the same. She recognized the impasse in her present collaboration with a man who helped her to continue repeating "I am not good enough."

Annemarie was too uncomfortable with her separation anxiety at that point to accept that she had no relationship and couldn't lose what she didn't have. She left counseling. Shortly thereafter, her abusive fiancé left her to take up with another woman. She got a sizeable amount of money from him in settlement of a palimony suit. She took the cash, had a complete body overhaul done by her plastic surgeon, purchased the first house they lived in together at an inflated price to get the occupants to sell, filled the house with every costly item possible, and continued to live full of despair.

All the acting-in and -out distractions Annemarie conceived of were not enough to keep her apart from the separation anxiety that seemed to be augmenting with each new purchase and each new surgery. Bringing herself back into counseling was the best investment she ever made in herself. Annemarie breathed a huge sigh of relief as she exchanged her purpose from separation through fear to connecting to her Higher Mind ... Until this point, she perceived herself as unacceptable to her God and all her troubles stemmed from this belief.

How could she find herself to be more acceptable to God? Forgiveness: the relinquishment of self judgment. She decided to shed the burden of self judgment and rather than constantly regard herself as bad, or poor, or ugly, she decided to simply be. She started to practice repeating "I Am", rather than "I am bad" or "I am ugly" or "I am poor". She suspended judgment of herself and simultaneously, forgiveness took place: forgiveness of her parents; her brother; her ex and, herself. Six months after practicing the release, some major shifts occurred in her life. She decided to get rid of some of the clutter in her house, and then she decided to get rid of the house. She got a new job, met some great new people with whom she felt accepted and worthy, she began to date an exciting new man. Forgiveness mends the **Spiritual Bridge**, effecting a connection to our Higher Power and inviting miracles of all sorts to take place.

When we have adopted someone else's version of who we are, we have to first become aware of that identity blip in our thinking network. What are some of your identity descriptions that have their origin through the words of someone else? Once you have identified that part, you then need to come to terms with how you have adopted and perpetuated that particular identity part as your own self definition. In so doing, you have removed yourself from creating your own definition of who you are. Releasing yourself from this ingrained way of thinking involves the conscious practice of forgiveness.

Forgiveness does not mean enabling someone who is into abusive behavior. We forgive a person, not a behavior. Many people think forgiving someone is the same as saying, "It is okay". Maybe that is why we are so resistant to forgive. Forgiveness states, "The behavior you did was not okay ***and*** in the name of my God, I love you." When we are spiritually connected, we are able to lovingly state our position to the other and are far more likely to have it respected and reflected back to us. If the forgiven person continues to make the same mistakes, we have the option to remove ourselves from the collaboration in fear and make that choice with forgiveness. Releasing with Love sometimes means moving on. People are so separated from their Spiritual Selves; we do not realize that forgiving empties us of fear and shame, making plenty of room for divine dynamics like creativity, courage, confidence, trust, hope, and faith in Love. Watch the external events fall into a healing frame of reference when we operate from a forgiving position.

Many times, in conducting psychotherapy, clients and their therapists as well, want to go round and round, ruminating about the past. These people are invested in being victims. Revealing the past is only useful as a means to gain a conscious recognition of the impasse that is re-created in the present. Once the spiritual breaks have been identified, it is no longer beneficial to focus on pain and suffering. What good does it do anyone to constantly concentrate on their childhood sexual abuse, their alcoholic father, their depressed mother, their parental abandonment, their victimization? What a waste of precious time.

Forgiveness is the release of the past. Forgive others as *humans in fear and in their own suffering* and forgive yourself for whatever hateful, angry feelings you've carried. Miraculously, many clients report a marked improvement in the quality of relationships they have with figures from the past, dead or alive, once they have practiced forgiveness. They stop recreating the painful scenario in their daily lives. They also report a sense of peacefulness, energy, motivation, and joy.

How do we relinquish judgment of someone else or ourselves for a painful mistake? First, we exchange our purpose. In order to make the exchange, we have to reframe the mistake from our Spiritual Self, not from our intellect, our body or our feelings. When we perceive through these last three states of Spiritual separation, we tend to place ourselves at the very center of the universe, with all things revolving around us. As a result, our ego is our god. In these states of separation, we are at risk to perceive certain things as intensified, sometimes to the point of grandiosity. When we work at perception from the Spiritual Self, we are empowered to experience a different point of view.

Ask yourself, "How would I know this differently, if I considered it from a position of Love, rather than fear?" In other words, "How would my God have me know this?" You can exchange your purpose of avoiding separation anxiety with connecting to **God in You**. Personally, the pain of one's childhood can be overwhelming from an egocentric position. It disappears when you release it with forgiveness. Our individual difficulties are only a microscopic glimpse of the pain and suffering the world has created at large. It does not serve us to aggrandize a meaningless memory so that it becomes a "golden calf", obstructing us from accessing powerful dynamics like courage, confidence, trust and hope.

> Sandy, a twenty-five year old law student, came to see me very shortly after her parents were divorced. She was referred to me by her mother, who had come for counseling right at the time her mother's husband left her after twenty-seven years of marriage. Sandy's mother had a history of depression, offset by episodes of rage that were terrifying to whoever happened to be present at the time.

Her mother's husband was having a lengthy affair with a colleague. He left the marriage because he was tired of caretaking what he perceived to be a non-functioning spouse. In their years together, he was constantly walking on egg shells around his wife, being the proverbial nice guy, and not rocking the boat. I don't believe, in all their years together, he ever simply asked her to cut it out because her acting in and out was hurting both of them and their two children as well.

Mom was a second born daughter and Sandy was a second born daughter, as well. Mother fared very well in treatment and terminated treatment with a home of her own, a full time job as supervisor for a four-star resort, and a sense of peacefulness and power over her life.

Shortly thereafter, Sandy and her partner went to a party with Sandy's older sister. There, she became very drunk and revealed to her sister that she was gay. Sandy, then had an intense argument with her partner, left the party, and hailed a cab to get home. She started conversing with the driver and again, reported that she was gay. After the cab passed the turn-off to her house, Sandy realized she was not going home. The driver took her to a desolate spot and raped her. Being drunk, Sandy was unable to fight him off. Sandy was in deep emotional crisis about these events and this was her presenting problem at the time she came in.

The part of this presenting problem that peaked my curiosity was that after the episode, she went directly home and showered for two hours. Why would a highly intelligent law student, who is an activist for feminine rights, destroy important physical evidence that would directly lead to the arrest of her assailant? The answer to this question cannot be found in the here and now.

The explanation was found once we revealed the history. In the course of growing up with Sandy's particular set of circumstances, she felt extremely frightened of her mother's behavior at a very young age. She also perceived that her father was doing virtually nothing to protect her. To distract herself from her fear, Sandy took on the protective role in the family. She spent exorbitant amounts of time being the perfect child and maintaining her mother's sanity. She would interact with mother for hours on end in an attempt to keep her steady. This was an exercise in futility, since we can never really be in control of someone else's sanity. Sandy was repeatedly only as good as her last performance. The pressure was constantly on her to keep plugging away and so she did. Unfortunately, this was useless to mother, who was enabled to never take responsibility for her own feelings and behaviors.

Once the divorce took place and mother took a turn for the better, Sandy believed she had no purpose and no identity. Behind all that, she carried a deep anger for her father, who she perceived as being very betraying and abandoning in his passivity toward Mom. She primarily struggled with repeating "I am valueless", a judgment she made as a child who thought that if she were of any value, Dad certainly would have watched over her. The memory of the rape with the absence of assailant accountability sustained her unconscious re-creation of male betrayal.

The fear and shame she carried from childhood flourished in the incorrect childhood perception that she in some way deserved her paternal abandonment. She judged that she was not lovable or valuable enough to receive any better. She wasn't acceptable to her God and this judgment she had perpetuated on her own. After the betrayal of rape, she betrayed herself by washing away important evidence. Once again, she saw herself as a victim who is powerless and out of control.

Sandy came to quickly understand this in our time together and she began to let go of her past through reciprocal forgiveness. She bridged into her own perceived void and realized it was no void at all. She understood it was a place inside that was originally meant for her spiritual self, something she had abandoned through her distraction of being the perfect child.

The rape is in the past. It is now a memory like all memories, which can be rendered meaningless through forgiveness. Sandy

> exchanged her purpose in counseling. She relinquished self judgment and in so doing, corrected her perception of the experience as a glimpse of a fear-based world where the choices seem to be: attack, be attacked, or take no risks and avoid it all. Her new purpose inspired her to extend **God in Her** to others. Incidentally, Sandy is now a syndicated journalist and writer. She perceives herself to be creative, gifted, talented and lovable. Her relationship with her parents is the best it has ever been.

Take a minute and reflect upon some memory that has resulted in self judgment. It does not necessarily have to be as dramatic as some of the cases used in this book in order to illustrate a particular point. Maybe someone else contributed to the story of your identity by helping you to believe you are something you would prefer not to be. You can shift your perception of that memory by stating. "That memory is not bad, it just is. Now, what do I want to create for myself around it?"

Releasing the past through the relinquishment of judgment begins mending the impasse in the **Spiritual Bridge**. Now that we have exchanged our purpose and therefore changed our minds, we are ready to use thoughts of peace to change our behaviors when we are being challenged by fear.

6

RESPONDING TO FEAR

It is the privilege of the forgiven to forgive.

I know.

There is a big difference between *responding* and *reacting*. Reacting involves little or no spiritual connection. It is ruled by the unconscious mind and is predicated upon our attachment to the painful past. To react is to act back or to act again and can become the re-creation drama of the impasse. Reaction is defensive in nature and is based on the physical instinct of fight or flight. We react when we have a need to protect ourselves. Sometimes this is desirable. If a car is coming right at you, luckily you will react by swerving your own vehicle out of the way. In the immediacy of physically threatening situations, the fight or flight instinct kicks in automatically and is not based on the projection of our painful pasts. Reaction skills are very useful should we find ourselves in physically dangerous circumstances.

Responding involves the introduction of a reply or an answer. How do you answer in emotionally fearful conditions? Most of us tend to use the same fight or flight reaction in emotionally fearful circumstances. That looks like either verbally attacking the fearful subject or withdrawing from it. In emotionally scary circumstances, neither of these reactive options is very useful simply because they breathe life right into the fear they are attempting to eradicate. Attacking someone puts us in the perpetrator position. Withdrawing from someone puts us in the victim position. Either way, we keep ourselves stuck in the drama triangle and we feel a lot of pain.

Joan, a thirty-year old woman came to see me because she was still on the fence about getting a legal divorce after a seven month separation from her husband. Joan explained that she was feeling afraid to make a decision. Being officially on her own seemed frightening and giving her rageful husband the bad news seemed equally as frightening. Joan withdrew from a scary set of circumstances and the more she withdrew, the more life she breathed into her own fear.

She physically lived apart from her husband for seven months while he continued to pay the bills, keep track of money, and keep track of Joan. Joan never really moved through any of the challenges of independent adult living and passed on the opportunity to build her confidence in taking care of herself. Joan also chose not to face the unacceptability of her husband's abusive behavior. His aggression was very frightening to her and her decision to check out from it actually reinforced his tendency to go after her, once again breathing life into the very thing that scared her.

Shortly after getting Joan's history, I reflected for her that making no decision about being married was in fact a decision. Either you are in a relationship or you are not. She thought she was avoiding a divorce. I believed she was avoiding the marriage and that was clearly a decision not to be married. Her difficulty was not in her apparent ambivalence; her difficulty was her reacting rather than responding to her fear. What was her fear? Her fear was of abandonment and that fear had its roots in a much earlier time.

When Joan was ten years old, her alcoholic, rageaholic father began to sexually molest her. This continued for about six years, as Joan was threatened in a number of ways by her father if she were to ever make a fuss or tell anyone. Joan was at her father's mercy for a very long time. Adding insult to injury, Joan's mother refused to believe and protect her daughter, when at sixteen years old; Joan mustered up the courage to tell her the sordid tale. Joan was trained at a young age to take flight from fear. She learned to withdraw and dissociate from fearful situations. She unconsciously re-created the history in her marriage to an abusive man, held herself at his mercy, and ironically abandoned herself over and over again by not responding to her fears.

After we ascertained that she no longer wanted to be married, her husband certainly escalated with inappropriate behavior. Joan commented that she was always afraid that he would react ragefully.

I then pointed out that her husband's abusiveness was his problem and not hers. She took on the responsibility for his problem because that was the position she took on with her father at an earlier time in her life. Joan recognized that her fear was the fear of defenseless little girl. She had until this point, judged herself as shameful and inadequate. When she relinquished self-judgment, she began parenting herself very differently. She calmly started setting very clear boundaries with her soon-to-be ex. She filed for divorce, opened her own bank and charge accounts, and served her spouse with an Order of Protection. With each responsive step she took toward emotional freedom, her fear shrank respectively. She reported a sense of peacefulness about herself and her ex as she let go. She began to build confidence and started to have faith in her abilities.

When we continue to allow ourselves to be defined, even in part, by historically painful memories, we are at risk to have the old fearful feeling states reactivated. Corresponding events in the present can be received in the memory part of the brain, which then triggers old, scary feelings. Neuroscientists have identified this type of worry circuit in the neuroanatomy of the brain. They have also identified that spiritual training, such as meditation, helps to shift this neurocircuitry to into a more beneficial feeling and behavioral outcome (Begley, 2007).

Responding to fear supports our release of the past. Once we have relinquished the self-judgment unconsciously made in a much earlier time, we need to stay peaceful when we meet up with a scary present day situation. We have committed to let go of the past. We have stated, "I can", which affirms our decision to no longer perceive ourselves as victims. When fear is triggered we can now state that we "know" what is really going on. We are right at the impasse and now know what to do so that we do not turn back. We meet and rise above separation anxiety, as we remember that we are not abandoned, not alone and we are worthy of our personal God's protective love. Responding, rather than reacting, implies thinking peacefully or calmly when we are deciding what to do in a scary situation.

> Burt, an investment counselor came to see me because at thirty-two years of age, he was lonely and had no relationship possibilities in sight. Even though he was successful at his career, he was unable to move past two or three dates with any particular woman. I put Burt into an empowerment group and about five minutes into his first session, I observed his problem. Burt was belligerent and came on strong with anyone who approached him. He reacted defensively in the most benign interactions, used a harsh tone and a forceful manner. He was downright rude to people. By the end of the first group session, members were setting all kinds of boundaries with Burt. They were rolling their eyes, and Burt was refusing to come back because he didn't "fit in with a bunch of losers!" Burt was afraid of connecting and letting people in. He unconsciously attacked them to hold them at bay. Incidentally, he was wonderful at it. I was truly surprised by his dismay at being alone, especially since he seemed to work so well at setting it up.
>
> When Burt was in his latter adolescence, his father announced that he was involved with another woman and he was leaving the family. Two weeks later, Burt came home from high school to find that his mother had sold their home that morning and was leaving in three weeks for an extended visit to Europe. Burt was spontaneously emancipated: his life and his living arrangements instantly became his responsibility, ready or not. Burt wasn't ready. He found himself in a small room in a boarding house, eating peanut butter sandwiches, and just barely finishing high school while he eked out a meager income form his part time job in retail sales. That was the beginning of Burt's perception of himself as a "have-not".

> If anyone ever knew that he was such a "loser", they would never want to associate with him. Burt was afraid of rejection and so he would fight to keep people away. Burt never healed from his earlier losses. He was so afraid of loss; he continually breathed life into his fear by aggressing and attacking to keep people away. When Burt was made aware of the break to his Spiritual Bridge at the time of his parents' break up, he realized he had since been reacting to the original fear of loss. As he utilized the dynamic of forgiveness to release the past, he became more energized to respond, rather than react to the historical fear when it was triggered. Burt decided to remain in the empowerment group and built some very close relationships with other members.

Have you ever felt afraid or insecure in a relationship? What is that fear about? Why are you afraid? Take some time right now and think about the answers to these questions. When these fears are triggered, what avoidance do you get into so that you don't have to feel the fear? Emotional reacting occurs as a result of poor impulse control. Our immediate impulse is to get away from the scary feeling because it is so unpleasant. So we impulsively turn to distracting behaviors that ultimately only serve to give fear reign over our lives. We abandon ourselves in the process by dishonoring what it is we are feeling. Instead, we camouflage the feeling with distracting behaviors that tend to get out of control and help us to believe that we are incompetent at functioning in the world. Acknowledging fear is required in order to respond to it.

> I started working with Leila, a forty year old female attorney, very successful in the business world and very unsuccessful in a fourteen year long collaboration in fear, she called marriage. Her husband, struggling with his own avoidance of fear, moved out after he told her he was sick and tired of putting up with her rage and intense verbal attacks. Leila was shocked at Jim's "impulsive behavior" of leaving, which she described as extreme. When she started counseling,

she insisted that Jim was experiencing midlife crisis. She wanted to spend her therapeutic dollar talking about how troubled he had always been and how she continually rescued him in their time together. She represented that she was not an attacking person and clearly, Jim did not appreciate how hard she had worked to make sure he was happy.

The first three weeks of our relationship, Leila would page me every other day. Clients are informed that paging me is an option only to be used if the client is in crisis. Whenever I returned those early calls, Leila would not tell me she was in crisis, she would act it out.... right in my direction.

One time, I received a page from her while I was driving an interstate highway to pick up my daughter from college. Leila paged me with the number to her cell phone and when I exited off the highway the first two times, she was not present to take my call. On the third try she was there and her question was, "Jim invited me to dinner tonight. Should I go?" I reminded her that when she paged me, the assumption was that she was in crisis. If she was feeling fearful about something, she needed to talk to me about that.

Another time, I was in a prayer meeting when she paged me and upon my call she pointedly asked, "Did Jim cancel his appointment with you on Friday?" I responded by stating that due to issues of confidentiality, I could not answer that question and if she needed an answer, why not ask Jim directly? I reiterated that when she paged me, she needed to be in touch with her feelings of terror and talk to me about that feeling.

Soon thereafter, Leila did not page me, but left a message on my voice mail canceling all further appointments. When I called her back, she stated with remarkable hostility that she needed a shrink who would be more "soothing and comforting" to her. After one or two information questions, she revealed that she had a very difficult weekend and she was afraid to page me. Leila was afraid to have and express her fear. Her impulse upon fear was to distract herself by going after people to make her feel better. This was fruitless because at these times, she would withhold what it was she was really feeling anyway. Instead, she would behave in a pushy manner, which pushed people away. Moreover, her reaction to fear by getting aggressive got her the opposite of what it was she said she wanted: comfort.

Jim was at the end of the line with being on the receiving end of unkind treatment, and quite frankly so was I. When I explained to Leila what I observed about her behavior, I concluded in stating that I would be happy to refer her out for a better fit and that it would never be useful for her, her therapy, or for me if she did not have trust in our relationship.

At that point in our conversation, she emphatically had a change of heart and wanted an extra session that week. Leila was re-creating some painful scenario from her past where the outcome appeared to be abandonment. Now that she was ready to get down to work, she revealed that she was raised as an only child in the swank Park Avenue section of New York City. Her father was a busy doctor who was rarely home. Her mother was a very beautiful and very depressed former model, who was over medicating herself with a lot of prescription drugs. Even though her mother was there physically, she really wasn't there emotionally. Leila was passed off to a series of nannies.

One day, her mother took it too far and died from a prescription medicine overdose. Leila's father never dealt with the tragedy and indulged her to try and keep her happy. Leila shared that her favorite pastime as a child was reading the Little Madeline books, which was a series about a French orphan.

Leila had deferred the experience of some very healing grief by feeling afraid of it and then minimizing the fear. Little Leila had lost both her parents, felt abandoned and that experience needed to be acknowledged and honored. What she would come to know is that the abandonment drama was always initiated with her own self abandonment by dishonoring her feeling state when it was fear on board.

Leila worked efficiently to feel her fear and experienced that nothing happened to her as a result of having her feeling. In fact, she became skilled at recognizing the feeling of a scared little girl who lost her mother through death and her father through his absence. Fear and subsequent self abandonment is always the backdrop for re-creation of the impasse.

Responding, rather than reacting, to emotional fear is the most important part of the transition to operating from love. It has been found that the brain's frontal lobes, usually regarded as the seat of higher order functions, forge powerful connections to the limbic system or the primitive brain (Begley, 2007). Responding is a discipline and it requires a lot of structure and practice in order to become efficient at it. Responding to fear is best developed by following three distinct behavioral steps: ***STOP, LOOK and LISTEN***. I remember this phrase being taught to me as a child when learning how to cross the street. That is a fitting analogy. Some streets are easier to cross than others. How many streets have you crossed when you never even bothered to ***Stop, Look, and Listen***? At some of the dangerous intersections, you could easily be mowed down if you didn't adhere to the rule. When you find yourself at a scary emotional intersection, the rule of responding is to ***Stop, Look, and Listen.***

Let's start with **Stop**. Identify what will become your personal red light. For me, as it is for many, my anger is my personal red light. When I am feeling afraid, my acting-out distraction from the feeling of fear is to become angry. Perhaps something is going on in my marriage that is triggering a historical fear or a break to my Spirit; I typically become impatient, frustrated, irritated, and angry. That is my red light. I ***stop***. I am obviously at a gap in my Spiritual Bridge, an impasse. I don't retreat back into the darkness of my ego and breathe more life into the fear, I simply ***stop***. Let me humble myself before you and share that sometimes I stop sooner than others, as I am sure my husband will be happy to attest to. But with repetitive practice, I am getting better and better at stopping sooner, which is a much nicer way to treat myself.

You see, when we are distracting ourselves from historical fear with various acting-in or acting-out behaviors, we are invariably the ones who suffer most. Ironically, I am finding myself at a place where my biggest problem of getting mad is becoming my greatest reminder of my need to respond, rather than react.

It doesn't take long to identify a personal stop light. Just make sure you never tell yourself, "I don't know" or "I'm trying" as you begin to develop this skill. The statements, "I don't know" and "I'm trying" are two of the most popular distractions to avoid dealing with fear. These two statements are a profound form of self abandonment that keep us stuck in the victim position, widens the impasse, and leaves the individual feeling powerless and hopeless. There is really no such thing as "trying" when we are making choices for positive change. We are either doing it or not doing it. We don't have to be hard on ourselves when we are not doing it, but let's at least be honest about it. Being honest with ourselves unblocks the path of forward movement.

When we ask ourselves the hard questions about our acting-in or acting out distractions, the answer "I don't know" is only feeding into our struggle with the underlying theme of incompetence and totally undermines our ability to respond to fear. Of course we know why, but if we copped to it we'd then take on the responsibility of making a change. If you are afraid to look at "why", simply say so as a first step in rising above fear. Stop and honor your feeling of fear. It is okay and makes perfect sense that one would experience fear in what is sometimes a scary world.

We always know in our heart of hearts what's going on with us. Stuck in the ego, we tend to be afraid to **LOOK** at it. Once we have stopped the distracting behaviors, we have freed ourselves up to look inward and reveal the truth in what is happening.

> I was working with a manager of a marketing firm who complained about the lack of loyalty with his marketers. The trend he was dealing with was that his staff didn't remain on board very long and many moved on to work with his competitors. When I asked him if there was some difficulty in his relationships with staff, he answered by saying, "Well, sometimes I get impatient." When I asked why he was impatient, he stated: "I don't know." When I asked if he was doing anything about his impatience, he remarked, "I'm trying to be more understanding." I then pointed out that if he wanted to work with me, he needed to understand that phrases such as "I'm trying" and "I don't know" were unacceptable.

> We then retraced our steps. Once he **stopped** his distraction of confusion and impatience, he then **looked** inward at the real story. Why did he get impatient? Because he was afraid his quota would not be met at the end of the month. He was repeating to himself "I am inadequate." This was a self judgmental thought he became invested in repeating to himself at a very young age. When he defined his impatience as his acting out to avoid his fear that he wasn't good enough, he could then hear the message being sent to him via an outwardly troubling situation. He **listened** peacefully to his inner story and realized he deserved to relinquish judgment: to be more patient with himself and others. The **listen** part is where we allow a thought of peace to enter our minds. After a little practice, his patience increased and the staff turnover decreased markedly.

Again I ask you, the reader, the question, "Why are you afraid?" Please don't answer with "I don't know." You *do* know. Just take a second and hang with the feeling long enough to feel it! If you would dare to stay with the scary feeling, you will soon discover what it means to you.

The enigma is that many of us try to overcome fear out of our egos, a system based in fear to begin with. For example, we might get very intellectual in our attempt to overcome fear.

We go to seminars, we listen to motivational speakers, we read self help book after self help book. We have a wealth of information but consistently tend not to integrate the information in a way that affords us the opportunity to live it out. Another example: we focus physically. We work out regularly at the gym, become nutrition enthusiasts, take yoga and eat yogurt. Yet, we still don't move ahead. Another pattern: we go to therapy for emotional growth and spend exorbitant amounts of time and money obsessing about the past and little changes.

When we can not integrate what we know to be true into what we *believe* to be true, we are at that familiar impasse in the Spiritual Bridge. When we consciously exchange our purpose from *maintaining ourselves at the impasse* for *bridging to God in us,* we can acknowledge our fear and separation anxiety because we are then empowered to do something about it. We can meet the discouraging feeling states because we know what to do when we're in them. We give the feelings to our Higher Mind and receive love in return. This inner transition is then environmentally mirrored for us through a series of corrective and uplifting events.

> Linda and Brent came to see me for marital counseling. I found it interesting that they would be seeking marital counseling, when for thirteen years they had yet to step into a marriage. They stood on the periphery of marriage because they were afraid. They each had become involved in extramarital affairs.
>
> Linda was withdrawn; Brent was constantly going after her. Each time Linda would stick her toe into the marriage, Brent would subtly shame her with some remark that would help her to feel inadequate. One such remark was, "There I am, every day breaking my back out there for my family and when I come home you have nothing to say to me!" Linda would remark back, "If I say something to Brent, he gets all over my case."
>
> I soon pointed out to Linda that it wasn't what she said; it was how she said it that was counterproductive. Linda made declarations based in fear. She would say things like, "Where were you when I tried to call you today?" or "Why else would you carry a change of clothes with you other than for a secret meeting?"
>
> When she was growing up, her father lectured her about how men simply could never be monogamous and how sooner or later all men cheat on their wives. He, of course had cheated on Linda's mother. He also objectified women in Linda's presence by cat calling to them and making sexual remarks as they passed by. This was a break to Linda's Spiritual Bridge because every time her father did this, he betrayed his daughter.
>
> Linda grew into adulthood unable to access the dynamic of trust. She remained withdrawn from Brent because of this historical fear. Brent, who carried his own fear of abandonment from an unavailable

mother, ended up firing Linda before she quit the job altogether by taking up with another woman. Linda took up with another man as a way to retaliate.

Unconsciously, both had inspired their early fears and re-created pain that had roots in a much earlier time. Linda would refrain from asking Brent for what she needed. She needed reassurance and commitment. She was afraid that he would never be able to give in this way. She then became angrier and angrier about not having her needs met. It was a vicious cycle, a distasteful collaboration in fear.

The most obvious issue around lack of trust was the struggle about the wedding band. When they were first married, Brent refused to wear a wedding band. He maintained that he didn't need a piece of jewelry to remind him of his commitment to Linda. Linda was very disappointed and scared about Brent's decision. After all, with the historical pain she carried, this issue fed right into her re-creation of the impasse. Brent made a bad call regarding his commitment. Ring or no ring, he ultimately stepped outside of the circle of spiritual union.

The wedding band issue came up repeatedly in session and the power struggle around it served as a distraction from the fear of commitment. Linda complained about it as a way to stay connected with her pain and when I suggested she request that Brent wear a ring because she deserved to have her needs met, she preferred to be in the angry place by stating, "I don't want him to wear a ring unless it is his decision to wear one on his own!" I further explained that it still would be his personal decision to wear one, whether she requested it or not.

I gave Linda a homework assignment to ask Brent to wear a wedding band because that symbolic act would be meaningful and healing for her. Brent indicated in the session that he would be happy to accommodate Linda.

> Every week for three weeks thereafter, they would come to session with Brent's finger still naked. Linda, 'comfortable' at the impasse, continued to refuse to make the request and she continued to use Brent's ambivalence as her excuse to stay stuck.
>
> Linda was entrenched in reacting, rather than responding to fear. We then employed the STOP LOOK, and LISTEN technique. Linda stopped the angry dance around the ring. She looked inside and experienced the sadness of paternal abandonment she experienced by father telling her she would be betrayed by a man. She peacefully listened to the inner message being delivered by what appeared to be an outwardly distressing situation: she was facing an opportunity to heal by giving herself over to a relationship of loyalty and commitment. Brent was hearing the same message for himself. I finally suggested that the mall was right across the street from my office and it would take minutes after the session to run over and pick up a small gold circle. Two weeks later, they came back. Brent was sporting a band and beaming about it. Linda was serene and satisfied. The basic portion of our work together was complete.

Here's a personal example. The first time I ever publicly presented a seminar, many of my friends and associates attended as a statement of support for my new endeavor. One of my closest friends was lagging in signing up. When time began to run short, I reminded her of the necessity of registering. She stated, "Ellie, I don't need to register. I'm coming to your seminar for you, not for me." I felt a distinct discomfort in my body as she made this statement. I discussed my upset later that evening with my husband.

I felt sad and disappointed. I perceived that one of my closest friends was showing up and declaring at the same time that I wasn't worth the price of a ticket. I interpreted mixed messages she was sending as a friend. I was bothered by the incident for a couple of hours. My husband suggested I practice what I preach and so I did. I asked for the meaning in what was happening, the meaning about myself. The answer came to me peacefully in a matter of minutes. I quickly remembered an incident that occurred the preceding week, where I had met with another friend of mine who was a very successful public relations specialist. I asked her for ideas and contacts to get attendees for my seminar. She complied and tagged on the end of our conversation: "You know Ellie, I don't usually work for free, but I love you so, there's nothing I wouldn't do to help you out." I left our meeting somewhat confused about her last statement, confusion being an acting-in distraction from fear. I soon dismissed it and didn't give it another thought, until I **stopped, looked, and listened** to the loving message about myself in regard to my other friend wanting a freebee for my presentation. The message was clear. I was receiving back exactly what I was giving out. I, in fact, did the same thing to my PR friend that was soon after done to me. I more or less told her that she wasn't worth the price of her time and expertise. I helped cause a break to her **Spiritual Bridge**. Breaking the **Spiritual Bridge** of others is something we can unconsciously get into as long as we remain unaware of our own personal breaks. The next morning I called my PR friend, apologized for my insensitivity, and asked that she would forgive me. She was loving, supportive, and our relationship deepened.

I felt calm and resolved about the initial incident that got all this rolling in the first place. The girlfriend who wanted free admission was a blessing in my life and I learned something important about myself as a result of what seemed to be an unpleasant experience. Listening from the **Spiritual Self** makes life much more interesting and much more enlightening on a day to day basis. We begin to understand that nothing is coincidental, that all encounters are meaningful, and what might have in the past been perceived as a negative experience can be reframed as an opportunity to learn and grow.

When we react, rather than respond to fear, we make fear omnipotent. It is in control of us, rather than us be in control of it. Fear becomes the altar at which we worship. It is a false idol. We choose to let it be the object of our faith, rather than choose some concept of God to have that position in our lives. When we respond to fear, we are using the God-given gift of free will to exchange fear for Love. When we make the conscious choice to make the exchange, we become peacefully centered in the **I Am**. As we enjoy thoughts of inner peace, we free ourselves to use wisdom in dealing with the distressing external situation.

> Matt was court remanded for counseling. He was arrested for exposing himself to two different women at red lights. He found this behavior to be particularly irresistible when he was at a light and there was a woman in a truck or recreational vehicle next to his car. He reported that if a woman was looking down at him, he was compelled to open his fly and begin masturbating. Matt had exposed himself to at least fifty women over the passed five years and the two who turned him in were gifts from God. They were gifts in that they offered Matt a way out of a compulsion that was destroying him and could destroy the lives of those close to him, including a wife and two young children.
>
> Matt's sense of powerlessness about this inappropriate behavior was, to start, the greatest thing he had going for him as we began to heal. The behavior was in control of him, rather than he be in control of it. Like any addiction, it was circular. Stuck in the unconscious purpose of projecting fear, he would experience a seduction into the acting out, he would act out, he would then be overcome with shame and self deprecation, which of course set him up for the seduction again because the shame felt so unpleasant. The sexually deviant behavior was not Matt's problem; it was his acting-out distraction from the feeling of shame and subsequent separation anxiety that had its roots in a troubled childhood. The shame was his problem.
>
> Matt was the first born in a family of three sons. He was a hyperactive child and was diagnosed with Attention Deficit Disorder when he was in first grade. He was put on Ritalin and was sent to a variety of psychiatrists and educational specialists for most of his elementary years. Matt always believed he was different and less adequate than the other kids who seemed to live a much less complicated life.

Even though his parents were going through the appropriate steps to help Matt out, they were very hard core in their discipline of him. They would beat him on the bare buttocks with a belt when he was being hyperactive. They sent him to a "Christian" school where paddles forebodingly hung on the walls of the principal's office.

It seemed, from Matt's perspective, that he spent a major portion of his childhood being punished physically and shamed emotionally. His father was absent a lot due to a growing and thriving business and mother stood staunch with discipline as she was left to keep a handle on three active boys. She was a perfectionist, who probably never came to terms with her own incorrect perception of Matt as an imperfect child. Matt's recollection was that his mother often spoke to him in a condescending manner and helped him to feel shameful and inadequate. A woman looking down on Matt was the trigger for his acting-out.

The day Matt began to truly reveal the history, he interrupted himself and began to cry. He told me that he was afraid to continue because he didn't want to think that he had bad parents. As if his own shame wasn't enough, Matt was also carrying his parents' shame for their own inappropriate acting-out with him. His scrupulous mother made it very clear that the family was to project the image of the perfect family and there would be enforced, a strict code of silence to maintain the image.

I let Matt know that his tears were the grief he felt about the loss of family through living a lie. I also shared that his parents weren't bad and very simply, they had made some mistakes in their parenting choices. It seemed to me that Matt was an easy distraction for Mom and Dad to focus on as a way to avoid some marital conflicts. Matt described his dad as a belligerent, verbally abusive guy. He added that his mother stayed out of her husband's way as much as possible and it didn't seem to matter to her if her husband worked around the clock. My thought was that it mattered very much and his mother chose to distract herself from it mattering by focusing her critical attention on

Matt. The history wasn't good or bad, it just was. Once it was revealed, Matt was immediately experiencing a greater sense of being in control over himself.

Matt recognized the impasse in how he relived the shame by attracting to himself a perfectionist wife who had a very revealing history of her own. The daughter of a paraplegic minister, she struggled with an enormous sense of inadequacy. She projected this struggle by continuously pointing out how Matt was not up to snuff in his partnering or parenting. Matt was defensive in the face of his wife's arrogance and once again, perceived another woman looking down on him.

Matt worked on releasing the past. He reframed his set of circumstances as an impasse in his Spiritual Bridge. The break to the Bridge as a child left him powerless to access the spiritually based dynamics necessary for joyful living. He learned the concept of forgiveness and gained wisdom from understanding its value. He forgave himself, his parents, and his wife. He became consciously aware when his separation anxiety was triggered. Instead of being lead into temptation, he employed the **Stop, Look, and Listen** technique. He understood that the idea of women looking down on him was an illusion he carried in his mind and he had the power to render it meaningless through exchanging his purpose. When Matt decided to forgive the self-judgment of shame, he was at peace with his parents and himself. His distraction of exposing himself no longer served a goal. His symptoms disappeared.

Here is a precious opportunity for you to take an intimate look within. Think about some aspects of your identity that you dislike. Stop judging yourself about them. The fact that you think, feel, or do certain things is not bad or good; it just is. Now what do you want to create around your situation? How about acknowledging and responding to your inner fear? You are now empowered to notice it, reframe it as an impasse, and then identify the judgment you have cast on yourself because of it. When we

Stop, Look, and Listen in a fearful situation, we empower ourselves to become very clear about what we are really needing so that an interaction can be fruitful, rather than fearful.

Volition and attention are two activities that can beneficially alter the neurocircuitry of the brain (Begley, 2007). Responding to fear is the exercise of free will for freedom. Spiritual exercise significantly raises activity in the prefrontal cortex of the brain (Elkins, 2003). This activity diverts neurons away from the fear center of the brain. Through spiritual discipline and repetition, we can build new neural pathways. This helps us to shift the way we think and enables us to rise to the intrinsic meaning of worldly suffering. We can then free ourselves from existential despair.

Responding, rather than reacting, brings with it the knowledge of our higher purpose, to extend Love. Once we know our purpose, we are ready to link up to **God in Us**. We are worthy and therefore, ready to receive and offer Love freely. Through this reciprocal process, we perceive ourselves correctly in the **I Am**. Here, we experience peace, courage, power, creativity, and joy.

7

RECONNECTING TO THE SPIRIT

Thus is your healing everything the world requires that it may be healed.

I Am.

Reconnecting to the Spirit is receiving our personal **God in Us**. Here is our moment of truth. Now we are ready to be who we truly are. Once we have moved through the first four steps, we are ready to complete the exchange. We have relinquished judgment of ourselves and others. We have used thoughts of peace to give fear over to the Higher Mind. We are now ready to receive our Higher Selves.

This is the only step that mentally requires we do almost nothing! Just be still and calmly listen. Simply be present for **God in Us.** Mending the Spiritual Bridge has opened the way. No longer invested in maintaining the false idols of distracting behaviors and having identified our historical grievances, we have moved beyond separation anxiety and we are ready to quietly receive the characteristics of the Spiritual Self.

This requires no concerted effort on our part, except a calm, attentive listening position. It is the accepting portion of the exchange of purpose. Spiritual characteristics draw closer to us as we reconnect. It is as if we attract them into our thinking. At this point, it is important to remember that a state of readiness to receive them is not the same as a state of mastery in receiving them. Readiness is the decision to receive these qualities as precious gifts delivered to us from our Higher Mind. Readiness occurs as we remember our true identity, called the **I Am**. Mastery is embracing the attributes so that they become the core of our identities. Repetition and practice in accepting these traits brings us to mastery of them. Practice includes activities that clear and open the mind: meditation and prayer are two possibilities.

Those of us who spend little or no time in bridging to the Higher Mind tend to complain that we have difficulty in relating to a personal sense of God. No wonder. We exert little or no energy in the relationship and then we are disappointed about it. God doesn't travel the Drama Triangle. We are not victims waiting to be rescued by a bearded old man in the sky. Furthermore, why do we receive something so great, so infrequently? It makes sense that for what we get in bridging, we would be doing it all the time. Bridging to the **I Am** or building a relationship with the Spiritual Self needs our input. M. Scott Peck wrote in <u>The Road Less Traveled</u> that in building a loving relationship, many times quantity *is* quality time. Devote some time to your Spiritual Self. You are worthy of it.

Reconnecting to the Spirit implies release of the past and response to fear or the application of forgiveness. When we have exercised this enough times, forgiveness tends to come to mind quickly and doesn't require much concerted effort. Think about how much psychic energy we pour into fear-based distractions, within ourselves and with others. If we gave a fraction of that energy into the discipline of Love, our state of mind and our interactions would be far more centered and peaceful. Imagine yourself feeling very irritated at someone else's fear-based behaviors and perceiving them as suffering in some way. If you were to regard this person with forgiveness, you might notice your irritation quickly dissipates and the situation resolves itself.

When we are peaceful in our minds, we take delivery of the clarity and energy of the **I Am**. This energy gives us the following characteristics: trust, honesty, tolerance, gentleness, joy, self-intimacy, generosity, patience, faithfulness, and open-mindedness. First, we utilize these characteristics unto ourselves. This feels so wonderfully liberating and powerful; we are enthusiastic to extend the same onto others. We then co-create spiritual alliances.

Trust is the first characteristic we receive as we let our minds be still. Having moved through the first four steps, we notice trust in ourselves as we remove the "Under Construction" sign that earlier stood at the impasse. We can let go of control and judgment. Our minds are peaceful and we trust that is all that is necessary to receive the power of the Spirit.

Self honesty is the essence of the **I Am**. Honesty can be described as consistency. It signifies the elimination of inner conflict due to what once was a need to distract ourselves through worshiping our painful pasts. It marks the end of self-deception or denial. Instead of self judgment, we practice self honesty. When we are operating from fear, we notice it, we don't judge it, and we then decide what we want to create for ourselves. Honesty proclaims our Self-acceptance and our true identities. Reconnecting to the Spirit keeps us honest with ourselves when tempted to stray off the path of Love. It is the motivation that reminds us to remember the first four steps when we meet up with separation anxiety.

Self-tolerance is the result of the relinquishment of self judgment. We now understand that we are *not* our behaviors. Honesty helps us notice that we have made an error. Self-tolerance protects us from going into a shame attack when we have made a mistake. Noticing that an error has been made now comes from an unspoiled awareness, not from a position of judgment. Free of shame, we give the error over to **God in Us** and thereby, invite wisdom in to handle the problem. Tolerance helps us remember that we are worthy to receive God in Us because we are not separate. Therefore, we maintain a position of being Self-accepting and letting Infinite Wisdom resolve the daily challenges of living life on this earth.

Gentleness is the inability to do harm to oneself or anyone else. When we live gently with ourselves, we make a conscious decision to not rebuke ourselves for our struggles. Berating oneself is the life force of any particular struggle. Self-harm is only an issue when one is invested in holding onto judgment as a way to stay separate and be 'true' to an insane belief that we are not worthy of connecting to God. Gentleness is strength and spiritually, does not imply the worldly connotation of passivity.

Joy is the awareness and appreciation of your goodness and inner beauty. It is the state we achieve when we are honest, tolerant, and gentle. Joy is different from the feeling called "glad" or "happy". Happy is the resulting feeling from happenstance or some pleasing outside event. Joy is the resulting state of the most precious inside event. It is a state of release that is free of fear, shame, and anger. As we receive joy, we begin to pay attention to our wonder rather than our woe. When we have met and risen above our separation anxiety, joy is what we experience in its place. It is a very powerful place to be.

Self-intimacy is experienced as a result of defenselessness. Fear nullified, defenses no longer serve a purpose. We are free of the need to protect ourselves against the context of a painful past, set up again and again. Defensiveness is what kept our symptoms as the altars at which we worshiped. As we receive intimacy, we state, "I could find out nothing about myself that would make me unlovable to my God." Self intimacy is the characteristic that compels us to extend Love to others. It is the mainstay of a spiritual alliance.

Generosity with ourselves is established as we reconnect. This is not the fear-based characteristic of greed. Greed is the fear-based result of being separated from **God in Us**. Greed is a distraction based in thoughts of lack and scarcity. When we are separate, perceiving ourselves as alone, we believe we have nothing and so compensate by keeping things for ourselves. Generosity with oneself signifies the quality of quantity time connecting to the Spiritual Self. Being generous with ourselves means receiving the abundance of God in us as much as we can. Ironically, when this generosity is received, we are driven to give it away to others. Generosity is the main dynamic that ensures we stay the path of Spiritual connection.

Patience with ourselves is received in the **I Am**. Since being in the present is the human experience of eternity, there are no time constraints and therefore, no need for impatience. No longer separate, we release the need to control things based on being the only man to do the job. Since we giveaway control based in fear, we gain patience within. Passion is the root word of patience. Patience is a passionate expectation of Faithfulness within and motivates us to give the outcome of any given situation over to **God in Us**. As we give a problem over, we receive knowledge in how we might become a vehicle for what we believe will be a loving outcome. Faithfulness gives us inner vision. When we use inner vision to perceive any particular event, we have faith that the event serves us by either protecting us or providing us with some new self understanding. We have faith that we will be spiritually served by the event, even if it doesn't appear that way in its original manifestation.

Open-mindedness occurs as we receive **God in Us** and with it, we are empowered to take risks, extend ourselves, and realize the talents and abilities we possess on a grand scale. We begin to see with a vision that is not of our eyes and believe that there are no limits to the possibilities. As we accept this vision for ourselves, we see the endless possibilities for others. Creativity soars, enthusiasm resounds, and courage abounds. It is the open mind that has the power to view miracles.

It is important to differentiate between embracing these characteristics and acting them out. There are some who get into what I call a case of the dog wagging the tail. They think that if they *act* patient, tolerant, etc., then they will be acceptable to God. This is not how it works. When we are in release of the past and have responded to fear, we are centered in the present and able to receive these spiritual gifts. We do not act them out, we become them.

I am a member of a bimonthly prayer group that collectively makes prayer for each individual member. One by one, we go round the table and as each member states their concern, they state it in very general terms. Initially, being the shrink I am, I thought each member needed to explore *why* they were facing certain issues of insecurity, worry, and despair.

As the spiritual leader simply began a prayer for a member, speaking from a higher level of consciousness, lending the problem over to Love, I realized that the "why" was very unimportant. What does it matter why you are upset? The only thing that matters is that your upset is not a natural state and once your natural state is restored to you, the upset is gone. Why try to figure out the reasons for something that doesn't really exist in the first place? When members of the prayer group state their issue, they invariably begin to cry. This sadness is the gateway to joy. It is through embracing our pain, rather than distracting ourselves from it, that we become empowered to rise above it. Reconnecting to the spirit is the decision to embrace your true vision, vision that is not of any physical form. It is the resolve to view any given situation from a higher level of consciousness and it does not involve seeing, thinking, or feeling. It simply involves being.... being one with Love, one with our sense of God.

How do we achieve this state of being? By going inward, deeply inward. You can explore and discover a vehicle for inner contemplation that fits for you. Here are some contemplative activities, other than meditation or prayer, you might consider: practice yoga; be in nature; engage in the arts; pray for the person you dislike; read and journal; cook a meal for someone; star gaze; help the sick; attend someone else's church or temple; exercise; do a charitable act; take care of children; play games; help the elderly; teach; read for the blind; participate in an ecological endeavor; join or form a spiritual study and/or encouragement group; give compliments; listen actively to others; pay attention; or express gratitude. These are just some suggestions. You may have your own personal path in mind.

Initially, when we reconnect to the spiritual self and seem to be doing just fine, something will happen that will typically shoot us down. As we begin to make the shift to the spiritual perspective, we may first experience the intensification of forces of fear as a way to bring us back to the familiarity of our suffering. At this point we are being seduced to slip back into the victim and to sell our souls.

At these times, if you remember to draw upon your faith in Love and bridge to your Higher Mind, you become a laser beam of light, transcending through every obstacle as if it wasn't there at all. After a while, you simply disregard the obstacles. Disregard means to honor no more. You can refuse to inspire or refuse to breathe life into the force of fear. You can eliminate fear as the object of your faith. Every time you feel afraid, the thought, **I Am** will be all you need to be just fine.

Ben came to see me after he viewed a movie where a man recovered memories of childhood physical and sexual abuse. He reported that he became emotionally overwhelmed during the movie and realized that something had been triggered for him. Ben was about to be divorced from his wife of twenty-five years. Her major complaint was that Ben was closed off, low energy, and never finished any project he started. Ben was an attractive, highly intelligent man with an eloquent command of the English language and a brilliant sense of humor.

When he was thirty-five, he was promoted to the position of vice president of a major advertising agency in Manhattan and three days after the promotion, he suffered a major heart attack. Ben boasted that he was written up in several medical journals as the youngest man to ever suffer so profound a cardiac condition.

One year after the heart attack, he had triple bypass surgery, left New York and settled in Arizona to lead a more laidback lifestyle. Laidback was an understatement because in the years since the move, he spent most of the time on the den sofa, talking about business plans that never materialized and complaining that his wife never had sex with him.

When we began our work together, Ben wanted to spend forty-eight of our fifty minutes complaining about what a cold woman his wife was. When, during our second session, it became clear that he wanted to sing the same old song. I asked, "What is your fascination with cold women?"

After Ben restored himself from what appeared to be a startle, he replied that his mother was the original cold woman, with a heart like a block of ice and a temper that was terrifying. She name called her kids some of the worse names one could imagine. She beat them regularly. She would be fine one minute and fly into a rage the next, for no apparent reason. One never knew when all hell would break loose, and so there was no sense of stability or security in the house. There were no hugs or kisses, no words of encouragement or love ... not a shred of tenderness. His father spent day and night at the family owned grocery store and when he was around, he wasn't much better.

Ben was the second born of two sons and for much of his early life, he observed his older brother be annihilated with some of the most perverse abuse I have ever heard about. His mother would force the boys to eat a large, heavy breakfast if they wanted it or not. One morning the older brother was feeling sick to his stomach. Perhaps he had the flu or perhaps he had the fear. His mother commanded him to eat. He tried to but he felt so sick. She screamed at him to eat. He put some eggs into his mouth and slowly began to chew. She screamed at him to swallow. He attempted to do so and with the attempt, he bolted from the table, into the bathroom, and began to vomit in the toilet. His mother charged in, grabbed the back of his head by the hair, and pushed his faced deep into the pool of vomit. The older brother grew up with many issues of his own, spent years in therapy, and finally came out to his wife of thirty years that he was gay.

Ben, witnessing many scenes like the one I described, built up a tall, thick dissociative wall to survive his childhood. The "wall saw him through. He was afraid to give it up long after he left home and had a family of his own. His mistrust of women was re-created with his wife, where he rarely extended himself and then described her as "cold". He was not present for his own two kids, except to write them checks, as his father did for him. His son was twenty four and was going nowhere in his life. His daughter was twenty two and struggled with severe sexual addiction. Ben's broken spirit was reflected in his fear of success and his fear of life itself. Ben's wife finally filed for divorce and moved out. A few days later, Ben was involved in a major car accident that almost cost him his life. The accident actually cost him several years and several surgeries before he would allow himself to recover. Ben was very "comfortable" keeping himself in a dissociative state and apparently went to great lengths to re-create the impasse. I visited him at his home shortly after he was released from the hospital. Upon entering the room, he looked up at me, smiled, and said, "Now don't start with me, Ellie. I didn't want to have a car accident!" "Sounds like you've been giving your situation some serious consideration, Ben", I replied. Ben's ability to laugh at himself was his greatest therapeutic tool and as we made eye contact, we both started to laugh.

As soon as Ben could drive he came back to the empowerment group he was working in at the time of the accident. With the latest sequence of events, he had literally brought himself to his knees and was now ready to pray for some enlightenment. Ask and it shall be given. Ben began to deal with the gap in his Spiritual Bridge. Watching mom and brother had Ben paralyzed with fear. His perception of this experience was so horrific he acted-in and checked out. He re-created this theme in many dimensions of his life. Ben came to realize was that he was ultimately checked out from himself and in so doing had robbed himself of a number of loving, healing relationships.

Ben had remembered his history in such a way as to perceive himself unworthy of love and affection. He didn't give any and he didn't get any. Ben's judgment of himself as unlovable and permanently scarred, combined with his judgment of women as untrustworthy and unkind had certainly played itself out to the max. Ben was invested in seeing himself as a victim of a broken heart until he learned about the role of forgiveness in mending the **Spiritual Bridge**.

Ben realized that he had been berating himself for many years. He also realized that he had been berating his mother and although she had died when he was in his early forties, she was very much alive and well in his mind. Ben made a decision to forgo judgment. His experiences were not good or bad, they simply were. He prayed about all the mistakes that diminished the quality of his life. As he prayed, he gave them and judgment about them to his God.

He had mended the Bridge and opened the way for wisdom to enter. Ben began to invest himself in wellness, instead of sickness. His health began to improve: he joined a Temple; he joined a gym; and he met a great lady. Ben made amends with his kids and took a consulting job with a PR firm. His protective wall came down and all sorts of wonderful experiences found their way to Ben.

When life's challenges retrigger our historical upsets, we are at risk to feel afraid and then distract ourselves from that feeling. Some of us have intricate distractions; some have more simple and obvious ones. Once we remember forgiveness (relinquishment of judgment followed with a thought of peace), we stop evaluating the intensity or nature of our distractions and become less analytical. We notice our fear and utilize our mended Spiritual Bridge. Connection to the spiritual perspective empowers us to stay centered and trustworthy of our ability to rise above any challenge life has to offer.

8

THE SPIRITUAL ALLIANCE

Make way for Love which you can extend.

When we have reconnected to the **I Am**, we are compelled to extend the attributes of the spirit out to others. This bridging to others is what I call a spiritual alliance. It is based in Love and sees a sense of God in the other. When we are spiritually connected to another we are aware of the good dynamics that flow between us. We take responsibility for our own feeling states and are motivated to lovingly state our position to the other when something is going on that does not fit for us. We can easily practice the act of forgiveness because we are not stuck in projecting our historical pain onto the other. Each person grows as an individual in a spiritual alliance.

One of the most popular spiritual alliances is marriage. When people marry, they name their relationship as a spiritual union. The basic spiritual difference between being married and living together is the vow or promise made in the name of your God, which pledges that two people will live spiritually as one. Marriage is an earthly expression of our oneness with Love, as symbolized by the exchanging of vows. Two people promise to be two spiritually complementary parts that form a perfect whole. Everything that differentiates you from your partner is what makes both of you together, spiritually whole.

The dictionary defines complement as "something that makes whole or perfect". I wish couples would remember this at the times they are conflicting over their differences. Many of them waste energy fighting off the very thing that makes them whole. They fight off what makes them whole because they are not spiritually allied and they collaborate in fear. They marry and then look for ways to remain separate.

A great way to respond creatively about our differences is to bridge to the Higher Mind during any conflict and ask oneself, "What is my spouse's behavior showing me about myself right now?" For example, perhaps you feel angry or sad when you perceive that your partner is not giving you enough attention or affection. When you bridge to your Higher Mind, you might notice that you, yourself need to show more affection to your partner.

My husband laughs everything off and I brood. We used to spend a lot of energy power-struggling over this. I would go after him to take things more seriously and he would engage by consistently telling me to lighten up. Each time we went around about this, we would step outside the marriage and give worship to our separateness. When we remembered what marriage is about, we could embrace each other's style as complementary parts, forming a perfect whole. A brooder needs someone to help them lighten up and a minimizer needs someone to help them prioritize the important issues. Together they can be far more powerful than if they stood alone. Couples who continue to power struggle over differences are into separation more than they are into marriage. At these times of power struggle, they don't have a marriage at all.

When spiritual union is the foundation of a marriage, the relationship is based in trust. An individual who has practiced bridging to the Higher Mind has received the gift of trust. When you have trust, you stay present for yourself and for the other without trying to control her/him. You are empowered to appreciate and honor everything that appears to be different between you. Trust that moves from the inner self to the relationship means you believe everything that is different between you and your spouse is a blessing that makes you richer and whole.

A common example of a trust challenge can be noticed when a spouse is concerned about the other spouse stepping out of the marriage through an extramarital affair. Trust is a spiritually based trait that starts within the individual. So, the frightened partner needs to respond to fear by relinquishing judgment and thinking peace. From this perspective, an extramarital affair is neither good, nor bad. It just is. What would you create around an affair if it happened in your marriage? The person needs to lovingly communicate to his/her partner exactly what their position is about infidelity, and what their course of action might be if it were ever to happen. Then leave the discussion in peace. This shift motivates the once frightened spouse to stay focused on remaining faithful for her/himself and stop worrying about what the other is doing. Whatever the other is doing is his/her responsibility. Your partner has heard your position on the subject. They will make decisions with that knowledge in mind.

Marriage is meant to be a spiritual relationship, not a special relationship. Couples are setting themselves up for trouble when they coin their relationship as "special". When we define the other as "special", we imply they are different or separate ... different or separate from all the rest. When we single someone out as "special", in essence we are setting that one person up to be on the receiving end of all our unreleased historical pain. We call them special and then proceed to project onto them all the hurt, anger, and inner conflict we may carry from an earlier time in our lives. Through this projection, we continue to re-create the impasse and therefore, inspire or breathe life into the painful past, keeping ourselves and the other in a consistent state of separation anxiety. Then, we try to distract ourselves from the anxious state by all kinds of acting-in or acting-out behaviors: extramarital affairs, domestic abuse, depression, physical illness, and divorce.

Marriage is the holy arena where you get to practice daily, hourly, love based behaviors. You check in regularly with your partner to reaffirm that you are both reflecting Love, enriching the spirit and extending that energy outward to other relationships. Practicing this in the sanctity of marriage heals the pain from the past and powerfully emits the same healing energy to the sphere of influence outside of the marital system.

SPHERE OF SPIRITUAL INFLUENCE

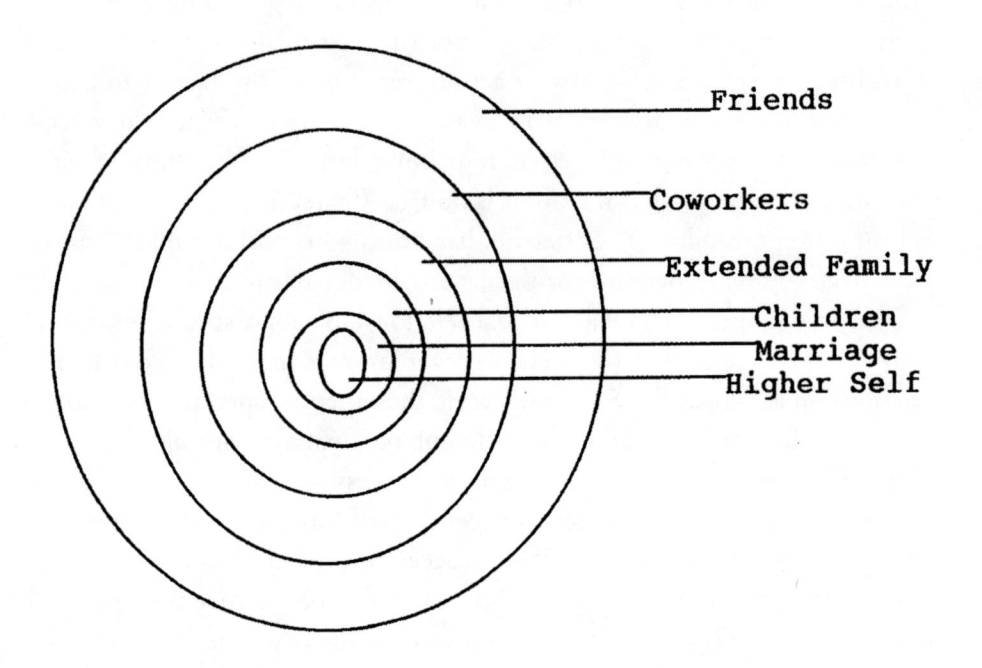

- Friends
- Coworkers
- Extended Family
- Children
- Marriage
- Higher Self

When we correct our perception of marriage from a special relationship to a spiritual relationship, our behaviors in the marriage begin to reflect that shift. Ironically, nothing is more calming when fear creeps into this holy union, than reminding ourselves that there is nothing special in this relationship. That understanding immediately helps us to make the conscious decision to refrain from acting-in or acting-out with our partner because if there is nothing special about it, we tend not to waste time and energy inspiring old hurts. We are freed up to make more useful here-and-now choices to keep the union sacred instead of special.

When the context of marriage stays spiritual, stuff that might trip our historical triggers has no impact at all. I worked with a gal who prided herself with her independence. As she made plans for a big wedding celebration, she shared with me all the omissions she was making in the ceremony itself. She was omitting words like "obey" and "serve" because she believed they would demean her as a woman. I pointed out that if she was stuck in perceiving her marriage as "special" instead of spiritual, those particular words would certainly cause her concern. If she perceived the marriage as a holy relationship, those words make sense. My husband and I serve each other spiritually and we obey each other spiritually … we team up to stay on the Love-based track because the purpose of our union is its dedication to extend the healing power of love outward through many surrounding relationship dimensions.

Partners in a special relationship abuse themselves and the other by trying to control things so that one will be what the other thinks she/he needs them to be as per their past experiences. Their marital environment then reflects the re-creation of the impasse through painful situations and heart wrenching events. Perceive a marriage as holy and watch the power-struggling disappear. Partners in a spiritual union spend their time releasing control and giving the relationship over to its higher purpose. They obey the tenets of Love and they are together to serve Love to themselves and to others. When they practice this, their marital environment reflects joy, abundance and peace. They look at each other and say, "It just doesn't get any better than this."

A Marital Mission Statement is very helpful when correcting our perception and making the shift from special to spiritual. What is your mission in life together? Is it to tear open old wounds and remain disconnected from all the powerful dynamics accessed through a clear connection to the spiritual self? Is it to collaborate in fear so that you draw to yourselves scarcity, loss, and anxiety? Research demonstrates that people who are made more secure through comforting, loving thoughts express greater compassion and willingness to relieve the suffering of another person (Begley, 2007). Imagine yourself in a relationship where old hurts are healed, and your energy does the same for your partner.

When we remember that our mission in life is to spread the power of the human spirit, we can also remember the power of the spiritual alliance. Whether it is within ourselves, with our partners, with our children or with the person in the car next to ours at a red light, it is thoughts of Love that heal us all.

9

THE PRACTICE OF BRIDGING: A REVIEW

Humans who struggle with emotional challenges have disconnected with that level of consciousness called the spiritual perspective. We did this at such an early age, we do not even remember doing it. Humans are born with this level of consciousness and then unwittingly disconnect from it as we encounter life in a scary world. The feeling of fear is unmanageable in early childhood and so we develop distracting behaviors as a way to cope. The distractions mature as we grow older, but we are spiritually stunted because we have not practiced existing from a higher perspective.

The spiritual level of consciousness empowers us to transcend the emotion of fear and offers the dynamics of courage, faith, trust, and hope to rise above personal struggles. When a person is bridged or connected to this level of consciousness, he or she is empowered to reframe life's challenges. When someone bridges to the spiritual domain he or she perceives him/herself as connected to a higher order of things and so, worldly experiences can be reframed as meaningful events that either provide or protect. As long as people are in spiritual disconnect, we are feeling afraid because we perceive ourselves as separate and alone.

Separate and alone, we live in fear and tend to react to scary situations by relying on the distractions that began developing very early in life. Grown up distractions are called addictions or false idols and maintain the impasse to the power of our spirit. Here are the five R's in brief, so that you can quickly review them when you need to be reminded that bridging to your spiritual perspective protects you and provides for you as you face the challenges of daily living.

1. Revealing the History
It Was

Your personal history is a powerful tool of insight for how you developed and how you presently and unconsciously react to events that trigger old fears and upsets. When someone is unconscious of these historical events, they will feel out of control when an old, negative feeling state is aroused by an event in the here and now that draws a parallel with an old piece of unfinished business.

Spend some quality time revealing your personal history. Reveal it as a chronicle, a narrative, or a story. Try to reveal it as something that once happened and is no longer happening. Reveal your history free of blame and accusations. Remember that the players in your personal history have histories of their own and bridging challenges of their own. The purpose of revealing the history is not to see ourselves as victims, but to empower ourselves to live consciously in the present.

Some of your personal history may be very painful for you as you reveal it. Simply remember that it happened once and it is not happening now. The pain you feel now is the pain you felt when it originally happened, but you never honored and resolved that suffering. You chose to distract yourself from it in childhood as a way to survive.

2. Recognizing the Impasse
It Is

Revealing our history, coupled with how we distracted ourselves from the fear we felt as children is a powerful tool for recognition of behaviors we use in the present to alienate ourselves from the spiritual part of our personality. These coping behaviors are hard to stop, because as children they were so successful in helping us deal with a scary world. Survival behaviors from childhood are hard to discontinue simply because they worked!

The Impasse can be recognized through ceasing an acting-in or acting-out behavior pattern. These patterns are addictive in their orientation. Once you have revealed your history, you will be able to recognize a place where you developed your particular pattern for distraction from feeling afraid. This pattern started as a childish habit and has "matured" into an adult distraction. Acting-out patterns include, but are not limited to, things like substance abuse, raging, arrogance, gambling, shopping, Internet, and other behavioral addictions. Acting-in patterns include, but are not limited to, confusion, depression, chronic illness, phobias, procrastination, isolation, running chronically late, forgetting commitments, religiosity, and giving someone the silent treatment. These patterns can also be described as worship of false idols in that they keep us away and estranged from our Godly nature. When you recognize your particular Impasse, you might notice that you feel some anxiety. This is separation anxiety: the scary hollowness we distract ourselves from as a result of being in disconnect from our Higher Selves. We are now ready to mend the **Spiritual Bridge**.

3. Releasing the Past
I Can

Our attachment to an unresolved past helped create the impasse that prohibits us from bridging to the powerful spirit. At this point of revelation, we can now stop distracting ourselves and release our original suffering with the divine act of forgiveness. Forgiveness must start with oneself. Our dependence upon our distractions has helped us to see ourselves as not worthy of Love. Forgiveness is a process that includes relinquishing judgment about a painful event, followed by a thought of peace. Relinquishing judgment is how we release the past.

The decision to release the past is a personal commitment to practice acting from Love rather than from fear. When we consciously exchange our purpose in this way, we can forgive ourselves and the person(s) involved and release the heartbreaking act over to the wisdom of the higher Self. Here is where we say: "The memory of the painful event that has me at the Impasse is not good or bad, right or wrong, it just is. The painful event is no longer happening. The only thing that keeps happening is my repetitive memory of it. My memory of the event consists of the event itself and how I personally integrated it. I'm not crazy, the memory is not crazy, and it just is." We remember that forgiveness is for people, not actions and therefore, forgiveness is a universal act. When we have practiced the process of relinquishing judgment, we are empowered to take responsibility for errors and grow as a result of making them. We can get out of denial about our acting-out or acting-in behaviors and reconnect to our powerful Spiritual Selves. We are now ready to respond, rather than react, to the feeling of fear.

4. Responding to Fear
I Know

Once we have recognized the Impasse and released the past, we will be much more conscious when we feel afraid. Now we have to practice, responding, rather than reacting to fear. Noticing and responding to the feeling of fear is what sustains our release of the past. We have already accepted the practice of relinquishing self-judgment. We have stated *"we can"* which means we no longer see ourselves as victims.

Now, when fear is triggered we state, "I *know* what is really going on here." We can be aware that in the present something has occurred which brings us to the Impasse, but now we do not turn back through our distractions. We meet the separation anxiety with a thought of peace because we remember that we are worthy of Love. Responding implies thinking peacefully or calmly when we are deciding what to do in a scary situation.

A simplistic tool for remembering to respond to fear is the phrase: **"Stop, look, and listen."** Identify what your emotional red light will be. For many, irritation or rage is their red light, the signal they are feeling afraid. For others it may be the blues or depression. What do you do to distract yourself when you are feeling afraid? You already have consciousness about it as a result of recognizing the Impasse. Become intimate with yourself and reframe the desire to engage in that behavior as your personal **stop** light.

Once you have stopped the distracting behavior, look inside to what is really going on. Recognize your impasse and remember how it estranges you from your authentic feelings. You are feeling afraid and you don't believe you can handle the fear. You'll quickly remember the history and the repetitive scary memory of it.

Now, listen to the memory with no judgment of it and notice the peace you experience as a result. You have just responded to fear. You are ready to reconnect to the most powerful part of your human experience.

5. Reconnecting to the Spirit
I Am

Once the impasse is bridged and fear is met, we are able to connect to our higher selves or **God in Us**. Mending the **Spiritual Bridge** has opened the way. We are now in a state of readiness to practice and master our true essence, the **I Am**. This requires no concerted effort on our part. The characteristics of being spirit connected appear to come naturally as we reconnect. We have worked thus far for a state of readiness to receive the attributes or gifts of the spirit. Now we can practice mastery in receiving them.

Mastery includes becoming practiced at noticing the forces of fear at work. We notice these forces and are not seduced to slip back into fear-based behaviors. Mastery means spending time in letting our minds be still so that we may receive the attributes of our Higher Level of Consciousness. The attributes of the Higher Self include, but are not limited to, trust, self-honesty, tolerance, gentleness, joyfulness, generosity, patience, faithfulness, and open-mindedness.

How you practice mastery in reconnecting is a very personal and individualized practice. You will create bridging exercises that work for you. Religion, or a particular style of expressing faith in Love, is only one form of practicing mastery. I have gathered a partial list of bridging exercises that may help you create your own path.

- Meditate.
- Practice yoga.
- Be in nature.
- Engage in the arts.
- Pray for someone.
- Read and journal.
- Cook a meal for someone.
- Star gaze.

- Help the sick.
- Attend someone else's church or temple.
- Exercise.
- Do charitable acts.
- Take care of children.
- Play games.
- Help the elderly.
- Teach.
- Read for the blind.
- Participate in an ecological endeavor.
- Join or form a spiritual study and/or encouragement group.
- Give compliments.
- Listen actively.
- Pay attention.
- Express gratitude.

When you practice bridging, you tend to see your God in just about anything you do and everyone you meet. Once you have become a master of bridging, the simple thought, "**I Am**" will be all you need to bridge to the spirit and feel calm.

People, who practice bridging to the spiritual self, become inspired to build spiritual alliances. We let go of the illusion of control and we lose interest in self serving activities as we become less ego-driven. We begin to form powerful relationships that generate spiritual energy and create miracles on many levels. We feel more intuitive and notice a lot of synchronicity in our lives. There is meaning in everything we do and we feel honored to serve others. This is the way we want and need to live.

10

A RATIONALE FOR THE PROFESSIONAL

Brief therapy is an umbrella term for a variety of approaches to psychotherapy. It differs from other schools of therapy in that it emphasizes a focus on a specific problem and direct intervention of a specific problem. In brief therapy the therapist takes responsibility for working more proactively with the client in order to treat clinical and subjective conditions faster. It also emphasizes precise observation, utilization of natural resources, and temporary suspension of disbelief to consider new perspectives (O'Hanlon, 1999). **Rapid Advance Psychotherapy** *is* a model of brief therapy that focuses on the specific problem of separation from the power of the spiritual perspective. It is a model where brief therapy techniques and spirituality converge. It is a timely and cogent model.

The advent of brief psychotherapy probably owes more to changes in the social, political, and economic environment then to progress achieved in theory or research. The Community Mental Health Act of 1963 and its refinement, the Mental Health Systems Act of 1980, lead to the democratization of the mental health movement. Popularization by the media, decrease of stigma, development of effective medications, decreased need for inpatient hospitalizations, the success of briefer behavioral and family system models of treatment, the shortening of leisure time with the advent of the two career family have all helped lead to the usefulness of brief therapy (Messer & Warren 1995).

Messer and Warren (1995) wrote extensively about a study of length of treatment. This study gathered data from counseling centers, health maintenance organizations, time limited and time unlimited settings, and community mental health clinics. When the experimenters plotted the number of sessions in relation to the number of cases remaining after each session for each of these settings, they found a negatively accelerating declining curve, which is referred to as the attrition curve. It existed across diagnosis, age, sex, presenting problems, ethnic features, and time limited or time unlimited treatment. It even held for individuals who were followed from one clinic to another. Furthermore, the study did not view the results as suggesting that the 'dropouts' were necessarily failures, but rather that many were satisfied with the help they received.

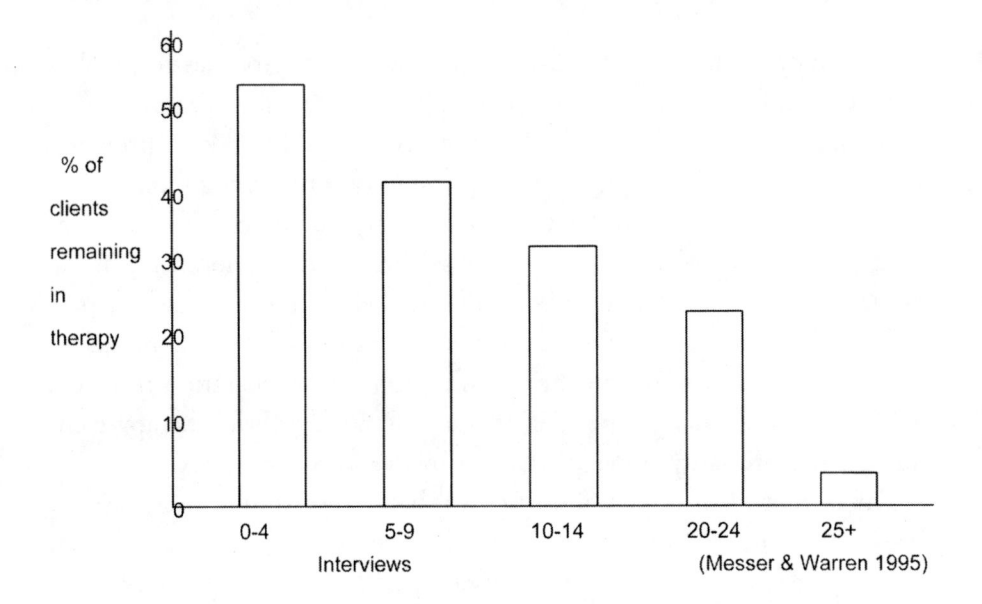

% of clients remaining in therapy

Interviews	% remaining
0-4	~53
5-9	~42
10-14	~33
20-24	~25
25+	~3

(Messer & Warren 1995)

Apparently, to a large degree, the client's attendance record sets the tone for the necessity of a brief therapy technique. Couple that with insurance offering reimbursement for a limited number of sessions and the clinician realizes that there is only a small window of opportunity to make a positive impact in the life of the client. Gustafson (2005) maintains that the clinician can make a difference in the client's life in only a few minutes. He believes that the majority of people seeking help from mental health professionals are not pathological, but are most often stuck in self imposed cyclical patterns of behavior from which they can not escape.

The assumptions of many traditional psychotherapies include: that there are deep, underlying causes for symptoms; that awareness or insight is necessary for change or symptom resolution; that amelioration or removal of the symptoms is useless or shallow at best and harmful or dangerous at worst; that symptoms serve functions for the clients; and, that clients are resistant to change and resistant to therapy (O'Hanlon 1999).

The assumptions of brief solution-oriented therapy include: that it is not necessary to know the cause or function of a client's symptom to resolve it, that rapid change or resolution of a problem is possible; that it is more useful to focus on what is changeable than on pathology; and, that it is healing for the client to find a trend toward positive change and encourage it (O'Hanlon 1999).

Milton Erickson was an originator and a master of brief therapy, using clinical hypnosis as his primary tool. The analogy Erickson uses is that of a person who wants to change the course of a river. If he opposes the river by trying to block it, the river will merely go over and around him. But if he accepts the forces of the river and diverts it in a new direction, the force of the river will cut a new channel (Haley 1986).

Brief therapy is often highly strategic, exploratory, and solution based, rather than problem oriented. It is less concerned with how a problem arose than with the current factors sustaining it and preventing change. Brief therapists do not adhere to one 'correct' approach, but rather accept that there are many paths, any of which may or may not in combination turn out to be ultimately beneficial (Hoyt 2001). There are now over 32 published research studies in solution-focused brief therapy which show successful outcomes, within four or five sessions, in 65–83% of cases (Brief therapy Practice 2007). The highest satisfaction ratings come from clients themselves and some of the research studies relate to very serious mental health problems, drug and alcohol use, criminal behavior and domestic violence (Brief Therapy Practice 2007). One such study followed the ten-session treatment of 97 widely varied cases. The findings demonstrate the achievement of significant success in 75% of the sample cases (Weakland, Fisch, Watzlawick, & Bodin 1974).

Solution-focused therapy is a brief approach to psychotherapy which explores current resources and future hopes rather than present problems and past causes and typically involves five sessions (Iveson 2002). Developed at the Brief Family Center (de Shazer et al, 1986), it originated in an interest in the inconsistencies to be found in problem behavior. From this came the central notion of 'exceptions': however serious, fixed or chronic the problem, there are always exceptions and these exceptions contain the seeds of the client's own solution (Iveson 2002).

The task of the therapist in solution oriented therapy is to find out what the person is hoping to achieve; find out what the small, mundane, and everyday details of the person's life would be like if these hopes were realized; find out what the person is already doing or has already done in the past that might contribute to these hopes being realized; and, find out what might be different if the person made one very small step towards realizing these hopes (Iveson 2002). The clinician makes use of the 'Miracle Question': a method of questioning that aids the client to envision how the future will be different when the problem is no longer present. A traditional version of the miracle question would go like this:

> "Suppose our meeting is over, you go home, do whatever you planned to do for the rest of the day. And then, some time in the evening, you get tired and go to sleep. And in the middle of the night, when you are fast asleep, a miracle happens and all the problems that brought you here today are solved just like that. But since the miracle happened over night, nobody is telling you that the miracle happened. When you wake up the next morning, how are you going to start discovering that the miracle happened? What else are you going to notice (Berg & de Shazer 1985)?"

Proponents of solution-focused therapy believe it can be effective with the most challenging clients because it fosters competence, empowers individuals and families, instills a sense of control, communicates acceptance, creates a context of cooperation, and transforms problems into opportunities (Rowan and O'Hanlon 1998). Although solution-focused therapy is a treatment in its own right, it can also be used to complement other treatments. Solution-focused brief therapy can help a client orient himself to other treatments that eventually will work (Berg 2006).

Since very large majorities of the American public believe in God: 90% in a Higher Power and 89% in miracles (Harris Poll 2003), spirituality is clearly a viable and positive client resource to be tapped into when using brief therapy. If spirituality is viewed as a sustainable resource by the client, even a non faith-based clinician can see the value in supporting the client to make the most of this internal resource. A faith-based counseling method which combines the best of non-faith-based counseling methods with faith interventions fits snugly into a holistic healing paradigm (McKinney 2006).

Until recently, many mental health professionals neglected aspects of religion and spirituality in their work (Young, Wiggins-Frame, & Cashwell 2007). Part of the explanation for excluding religion and spirituality from clinical work came from the conflict between the scientific, objective perspective of psychology and the transcendent, subjective aspects of religion (Burke *et al*, 1999; Lovinger, 1984; Pattison, 1978; Prest & Keller, 1993; Reisner & Lawson, 1992; Wallwork & Wallwork, 1990).

In addition, with the exception of pastoral counselors, few mental health practitioners have received formal training in working with religious and spiritual issues (Young *et al* 2007). In fact, Kelly (1994) found that only 25% of 341 accredited and non accredited counselor education programs reported that spirituality and religious issues were included as a course component. M. Scott Peck (1993) wrote about the predicament of American psychiatry. He called it a predicament because its traditional neglect of the issue of spirituality has led to five broad areas of failure: occasional, devastating misdiagnosis, not infrequent mistreatment, an increasingly poor reputation, inadequate research and theory; and a limitation of psychiatrist's own personal development.

Despite the fact that many counselors do not receive formal training in working with clients' religious and spiritual issues, surveys reveal that approximately 75% of Americans report that spirituality is important to them (University of Pennsylvania 2003). An increasing body of research suggests that spirituality and religion are often important family strengths. Various measures of religion and spirituality are associated with lower rates of divorce, greater marital satisfaction, higher levels of marital commitment, and greater use of adaptive communication skills (Hodge 2005).

Surveys of various client and potential client populations suggest that many, if not most, clients want to have their spiritual beliefs and values incorporated into the therapeutic dialogue (Bart, 1998; Larimore, Parker, & Crowther, 2002; Mathai & North, 2003; Rose, Westefeld, & Ansley, 2001). Furthermore, counselors themselves report spiritual and religious beliefs comparable with those of the general population. Omitting issues of spirituality in counseling is a choice to ignore a vital aspect of clients' lives (Young *et* al 2007).

A survey taken of counselors regarding attaining spiritual competencies provides evidence that a sizable portion (68%) of counselors do believe that such competencies are important to counseling practice (Young *et al* 2007). Part of the training therapists need to explore is their countertransference responses to spirituality. Many of us suffered in our childhood and later years to heavy handed religious teaching and this can lead us to regard all religion and all spirituality as harmful and unnecessary. It is imperative that we, as professionals, monitor our own resistances, countertransference issues, and value systems regarding spiritual issues if we are to meet ethically and efficaciously the special needs of our clients (West 2000). Additionally, training opportunities now need to extend beyond self awareness components to include training that provides opportunities to understand conceptual models and intervention techniques (Young *et al* 2007).

We have recognized so far that brief therapy is the model preferred by clients and that this type of treatment does not ruminate upon the problem, but focuses on building upon the clients' strengths. We have also understood that people regard their spirituality as critically important to them and that therapists need to recognize this fact and the implications it has for their work. It is time to consider spirituality as a paradigm in brief therapy.

Spirituality seems to be one of those words, like 'love', that has great importance to a great many people, but whose meaning is hard to pin down. The word spirituality is given a range of meanings within therapy and therapy related literature, varying from all forms of self awareness which possess values higher than average. Personal development as a whole is regarded by some as spiritual (West 2000), as well as therapy, itself (O'Hanlon 1999).

In the mid 1980's at Pepperdine University, a team of researchers decided to explore spirituality from a humanistic perspective and came up with this definition: Spirituality, which comes from the Latin spiritus, meaning 'breath of life', is a way of being and experiencing that comes through awareness of a transcendent dimension and that is characterized by certain identifiable values in regard to self, other, nature, life, and whatever one considers to be the ultimate (West 2000).

There are universal reasons why therapists should conduct a spiritual assessment of their clients. They are: 1) that it will help the therapist to better understand the clients' world views and thereby aid empathic understanding; 2) that it enables the therapist to assess whether the clients' spiritual orientation is healthy or not and to determine its impact on their presenting problems; 3) that it helps determine whether the clients' spiritual beliefs and community can be a resource for healing; 4) that it enables the therapist to determine which, if any, spiritual interventions in therapy could be helpful to the client; and, 5) that it enables the therapist to determine whether the client has unresolved spiritual doubts, concerns, or needs that should be addressed in their therapy (West 2000).

When people are intruded upon physically, experientially, or emotionally earlier on in their lives, before they develop a coherent sense of self, one can actually tell them what they are feeling and who they are and they will believe it. When that happens early on, the person doesn't develop a really good sense of identity, or some pieces get left out of the 'self' story that are actually in a person's experience. They dissociate from that and even more, they disown and devalue it. The identity self is the one that constructs "who I Am" (O'Hanlon 1999). When someone is in disconnect from their true identity, they can not remember or utilize the power of their life force or spiritual perspective.

Spiritual interventions heal, sometimes when traditional psychotherapy fails, because they untie the historical mental and emotional knots that prevent the life force from doing its work (Allender 1984). Donald Meichenbaum reported in an interview that with primary upsets, there are often secondary sequelae such as depression, interpersonal distrust, and addictive behaviors that have to be addressed as well (Hoyt 2001).

A team of Swedish researchers has found that the presence of a receptor that regulates general serotonin activity in the brain correlates with people's capacity for transcendence, the ability to apprehend phenomena that cannot be explained objectively. Scientists have long suspected that serotonin influences spirituality because drugs known to alter serotonin such as LSD also induce mystical experiences. But now they have proof from brain scans linking the capacity for spirituality with a major biological element. Those whose brain scans showed the most receptor activity proved on personality tests to have the strongest proclivity to espouse a spiritual perspective (Elkins 2003). Elevating serotonin levels will positively influence the clients' ability to utilize spiritually based behaviors.

Don Allender (1984) explains that to live is to hurt and the client is unaware of what to do with the pain. If he or she fails to respond appropriately to the wounds that life and relationships inflict, the pain will be wasted, it will numb or destroy. But he goes on to remind us that clients' suffering doesn't have to mangle their heart and rob them of joy. Healing is not the resolution of their past, it is the use of their past to draw them into deeper relationships with their God. Refuse to face the damage; the dysfunctional patterns set in motion to handle it will continue to exacerbate the wound.

Bill O'Hanlon (2003) discussed the three C's of integrating spirituality into brief therapy:

1) **Connection** by moving from beyond the little isolated ego into connection with something bigger;

2) **Compassion** or softening toward oneself or others by 'feeling with' rather than being against yourself or others; and,

3) **Contribution** by being of unselfish service to others.

He also poses basic assumptions of a spiritual approach:

- People are not defined or determined by the circumstances of their lives. There is more to people than nature or nurture, personality, genetics, biochemistry, or cause and effect.
- People have spiritual resources, even when they are not religious or when they profess no spiritual sensibilities or beliefs.
- Therapists can bring a spiritual sensibility into therapy without imposing it on clients.
- People have already developed ways of tapping into a sense of something bigger than themselves.
- Drawing upon spiritual resources can facilitate therapeutic outcomes.
- Religion is distinct from spirituality.

Spirituality, according to the Dalai Lama, is a highly refined tradition, perfected over 2,500 years by analyzing and investigating the inner world of the mind in order to transform mental states and promote happiness. He believes that psychology and neuroscience have gone about as far as they can go in understanding the mind by measuring external reality. Buddhism uses intelligence to control emotions. Through meditative and spiritual practices, awareness can be trained and focused to channel away from the kind of chain reaction of negative feeling, thinking, and behavior that has its own rapidity and inevitability. There is also astounding new research scientifically demonstrating that the consistent practice of spiritual techniques, such as meditation, contemplation, and prayer can literally change the structure of the subject's brain into a beneficial neural circuitry (Begley 2007).

The field of counseling will be served well with the model of **Rapid Advance Psychotherapy**. The model is brief, yet it offers the clinician a brief alternative that does not place a band-aid over a seemingly gaping emotional wound. The model is brief, yet it honors the client's underlying historical struggle without ruminating about it. It reviews the history to generate client awareness of the *impasse* or the disconnect from the spiritual point of view. It demonstrates how the client plays out the historical struggle repeatedly in the present through distracting, cyclical behaviors. It offers the client positive, easy, resource building skills to reframe the 'problem' and **bridge** to the healing, peaceful, spiritual perspective (Izzo 1994). Here is an excerpt from A *Course in Miracles* workbook lesson that exemplifies the reframe and bears a notable resemblance to the 'Miracle Question.'

Let me recognize the problem so it can be solved

- A problem cannot be solved if you do not know what it is. Even if it is really solved already you will still have the problem because you will not recognize that it has been solved. This is the situation of the world. The problem of separation, which is really the only problem, has already been solved. Yet the solution is not recognized because the problem is not recognized.

- Everyone in the world seems to have his own special problems. Yet, they are all the same, and must be recognized as one if the one solution that solves them all is to be accepted. Who can see that a problem has been solved if he thinks the problem is something else? Even if he is given the answer, he cannot see its relevance.

- In our longer practice periods today we will ask what the problem is, and what the answer to it is. We will not assume that we already know. We will try to free our minds of all the many different kinds of problems we think we have. We will try to realize that we have only one problem, which we have failed to recognize. We will ask what it is, and wait for the answer. We will be told. Then we will ask for the solution to it. And we will be told (p141).

The client leaves brief therapy with internal tools 'to face the forces of the river, divert it in a new direction and create new channels' for a healthier sense of Self. Once the client has completed the five sessions, he/she does not necessarily need to return to therapy to continue improving. The client can create a personal, ongoing spiritual journey that resonates. The client can **bridge** *to* these powerful spiritual resources at any time of upset and experience relief. The author respectfully encourages the clinician to creatively use the **five R's** of ***Rapid Advance*** for him or herself as well as for the client.

11
REFERENCES

Allender, D. (1984). *The Healing Path: How the Hurts in Your Past Can Lead You to a More Abundant Life. CO:* Water Brook Press.

Bart, M. (1998). Spirituality in counseling finding believers. *Counseling Today*, 41(1), 6.

Beattie, M. (1986). *Codependent No More.* MI: Hazelden.

Begley, Sharon. (2007). *Train Your Mind, Change Your Brain.* NY: Ballantine Books.

Berne, Eric. (1964) *The Games People Play.* NY: Ballantine Books

Berg, I. de Shazer, S. (1985). *Keys to Solution in Brief Therapy.* NY: Norton.

Berg, I. (2006). *Solution Focused Brief Therapy: Student's Corner.* Google: Online 8/24/06. [http://www.brief therapy.org/insoo].

Brief Therapy Practice. (2007). Research Evidence. Google: Online. 2/19/07. [http://www.brief therapy.org.uk/research.php].

Burke, M., Hackney, H., Hudson, P., Miranti, J., Watts, G., & Epp, L. (1999), Spirituality, religion, and CACREP curriculum standards. *Journal of Counseling and Development,* 77, 251–257.

Burns, D. (1999). *The Feeling Good Handbook.* NY: Penguin.

De Shazer, S., Berg, I., Lipchik, E. (1986). Brief therapy: focused solution development. *Family Process.* 25, 207–221.

Elkins, David. (2003). Of serotonin and spirituality. Psychology *Today,* Google: Online 9/12/06. [http.//www. psychology today. com/articles].

Goleman, D. (1995). *Emotional Intelligence.* NY:Bantam.

Gustafson, J. (2005). *Very Brief Psychotherapy. CA:* Taylor & Francis.

Harris Poll #11. (2003) *The Religious Beliefs of Americans.* Google: Online 2/20/07 [http.//www.Harris interactive.com/harris_poll].

Haley, J. (1986). *Uncommon Therapy: The Psychiatric Techniques of Milton Erickson.* NY: Norton.

Hendrix, Harville. (1990). *Getting the Love You Want.* NY: Harper and Row.

Hodge, D. (2005). Spiritual assessment in marital therapy. *Journal of Marital and Family Therapy.* Google: Online. 2/19/07.[http.//www.find articies.com/p/articles].

His Holiness the Dalai Lama. (1997). Love and Compassion in *For the Love of God: Handbook for the Spirit.* Carlson, R. and Shield, B. eds., NY: MJF Books, 179–185.

Hoyt, M. (2001). *Interview with Brief Therapy Experts.* Philadelphia: Brunner Mazel.

Iveson, C. (2002). Solution-focused therapy. *Advances in Psychiatric Treatment.* 8, 149–157.

Izzo, E. (1994). Managed Care: Burden or Blessing? *Guidepost.* 48(8), 6.

Karen, R. (1998). *Becoming Attached: First Relationships and How They Shape Our Capacity to Love.* NY: Oxford University Press.

Kelly, E. (1994). Counselor preparation: the role of religion and spirituality in counselor education: a national survey. *Counselor Education and Supervision.* 33, 227–237.

Kelly, E. (1995). *Spirituality and Religion in Counseling and Psychotherapy.* Alexandria VA: American Counseling Association.

Larimore, W., Parker, M., & Crowther, M. (2002). Should clinicians incorporate positive spirituality into their practices? What does the evidence say? *Annals of Behavioral Medicine,* 24, 69–73.

Lovinger, R. (1984). *Working with Religious Issues in Therapy.* NY: Jason Aronson.

Mathai, J. & North, A. (2003). Spiritual history of parents of children attending a child and adolescent mental health service. *Australian Psychiatry.* 11, 172–174.

Marano, H. (2003). Buddhism and the blues. Psychology Today. Google: Online. 9/12/06. [http.//psychology today.com/articles].

Messer, S. & Warren, S. (1995). *Models of Brief Psychotherapy. NY:* Guilford Press.

McKinney, R. (2006). *Introducing Rational Emotive Spiritual Therapy: A 2, 000 Year Old Spiritual Paradigm.* Google: Online. 8/3/06.[http://www.resr.com/art27].

O'Hanlon, W. (1999). *Evolving Possibilities.* PA: Brunner Mazel.

O'Hanlon. W. (2003) The integration of spirituality and brief therapy. *National Conference of the American Psychotherapy Association, The American Association of Integrative Medicine, and the American College of Wellness.* Aug. 22–24, 2003.

Pattison, E. (1978). Psychiatry and religion circa 1978: an analysis of a decade. *Pastoral Psychology.* 27, 147–199.

Peck, M. S. (1993). *Further Along the Road Less Traveled. The Unending Journey Toward Spiritual Growth.* NY: Simon & Schuster.

Prest, L. & Kekker, J. (1993). Spirituality and family therapy: spiritual beliefs, myths, and metaphors. *Journal of Marital and Family Therapy.* 19, 137–148.

Reisner, A. & Larson, P. (1992). Psychotherapy, sin, and mental health. *Pastoral* Psychology. 40, 303–311.

Rose, E., Westefeld, J., & Ansley, T. (2001). Spiritual issues in counseling. *Journal of Clinical* Psychology. 48, 61–71.

Rowan, T. & O'Hanlon, W. (1998). *Solution Oriented Therapy for Chronic and Severe Mental Illness. NY:* John Wiley & Sons.

Schore, A. (2003). Advances in neuropsychoanalysis attachment theory and trauma research. *Psychoanalytic Inquiry.* 22. 433–484.

Schucman, H. & Thetford. (1975), W. *A Course in Miracles.* CA: Foundation for Inner Peace.

Siegel, D. (1999). *The Developing Mind: Toward a Neurobiology of Interpersonal Experience.* NY: Guilford.

Titelman. P. (1998). *Clinical Applications of Bowen Family Systems Theory.* NY: Haworth Press.

University of Pennsylvania (2003). *New Penn/Gallup Poll measures "Spiritual state of the Union."* Philadelphia.

Wallwork, E. & Wallwork, A. (1990). "Psychoanalysis and Religion: a Historical Antagonism" in J. Smith & S. Handelman (Eds.). *Psychoanalysis and Religion.* (pp 160–173). Baltimore: Johns Hopkins University Press.

West, W. (2000). *Psychotherapy and Spirituality. Crossing the Line Between Therapy and Religion.* CA: Sage.

Young, J., Wiggins-Frame, M. & Cashwell, C. (2007). Spirituality and counselor competence: a national survey of American Counseling Association Members. *Journal of Counseling and Development.* 85(l), 45–52.

ABOUT THE AUTHOR

Ellie Izzo, LPC, PhD

Ellie Izzo has more than thirty years experience as a therapist, author, and public speaker. She developed Rapid Advance Psychotherapy, a standardized five-session brief model of counseling, that was presented at the American Counseling Association Convention in Atlanta, GA in 1997, and in Honolulu, HI in 2008. Ellie is presently collaborating on the books Second Hand **Shock: Vicarious Trauma and Its Treatment** and **Aftershock: the Workbook.** These books are for professional helpers and utilize the Rapid Advance Technique in the treatment of Vicarious Trauma. Ellie has hosted a popular Phoenix call-in radio show and served as Self-Help Editor for a nationally syndicated trade magazine. She runs several ongoing groups, the **Encouragers**, where people meet to offer each other peace, support and acceptance. Ellie is married with children and grandchildren. Her office is located in Scottsdale, Arizona.

978-0-595-46892-8
0-595-46892-6